EXPRESS NEWSPAPERS

non-retirement guides

your
home

How to reduce bills and
raise money on your home

Edited by Frances Kay

**KOGAN
PAGE**

First published in Great Britain in 2009 by Kogan Page Limited

Kogan Page Limited
120 Pentonville Road
London N1 9JN
United Kingdom
www.koganpage.com

© Kogan Page, 2009

British Library Cataloguing in Publication Data

A CIP record for this book is available from the British Library.

ISBN 978 0 7494 5586 6

Typeset by Jean Cussons Typesetting, Diss, Norfolk
Printed and bound in Great Britain by MPG Books Ltd, Bodmin, Cornwall

Contents

Introduction

Home sweet home is what matters to most people, especially
as they grow older. One of the most important decisions to
be taken as you approach retirement is whether to make
changes about where you live or to keep the status quo. To
many people, one of the biggest attractions once they've
finished work, is the pleasure of being able to move home.
No longer tied to an area within easy commuting distance
they can indulge their long-held plans of living in a new area
(possibly a new country). Although this could turn out to be
everything they desire, without any real assessment of the
pros and cons, some do regret having made hasty decisions.
It is sensible at least to examine the various options. An
obvious possibility is to stay where you are and perhaps
adapt your present home to make it more suitable for your
requirements. You might decide to move nearer to family or
friends. Or, looking further ahead, you could consider

buying or renting some form of purpose-built retirement accommodation.

Lots of people are conditioned towards thinking of retirement as being the time for selling up and relocating. An all-too-common mistake is for people to retire to a place where they once spent an idyllic holiday, perhaps 15 or 20 years previously, without further investigation. Resorts that are glorious in mid-summer can be bleak and damp in winter. They can also be pretty dull when the tourist season is over. Equally, many people sell their house and move somewhere smaller without sufficient thought. It may be that spending more time at home they will want more space, rather than less. This is particularly true of anyone who wishes to pursue a hobby that requires a separate workroom.

Although moving may be the right solution for some, especially if you want to realise some capital to boost your retirement income, there are plenty of ways of adapting a house to make it more convenient and labour-saving. Likewise, you may be able to cut the running costs, for example with better insulation. Before you come to any definite decision, you should ask yourself a few down-to-earth questions and be honest when answering them.

What are your main priorities? Do you want to be closer to your family? Would a smaller, more manageable home be easier for you to run – and less expensive? What about realising some capital to provide you with extra money for your retirement? How about living in a specific town or village, which you know you like and where you have plenty of friends? Or does the security of being in accommodation that offers some of the facilities you may want as you become older, such as a resident caretaker and the option of having some of your meals catered for, appeal to you? Whatever choice you make is bound to have advantages and drawbacks – life is full of compromise. But it is important that you weigh up the pros and cons carefully, so that you don't end up making a decision that – although attractive in the short term – you regret later on.

1

Staying put or moving

Staying put

With the property market in decline at the present time, there is a huge rise in the number of householders opting to improve rather than move. If you're a homeowner who needs more space, it makes sound common sense to extend rather than sell up in the current climate. House prices are predicted to fall over the next year and beyond, so many people's instinct is to sit tight. Instead of looking in estate agents' windows, the urge may be to look in the *Yellow Pages* for builders and decorators.

There may be plenty of arguments for moving and there are probably just as many for staying where you are. Moving house can be a traumatic experience at the best of times, and even more so as you become older. Emotional ties are harder to break and precious possessions more painful to part with, as is usually necessary, especially if moving somewhere smaller.

Although ideally you may want to remain where you are, it could be that your home is really too large or inconvenient for you to manage in the future. However, before you heave your last sigh of regret and put it on the market, it is worth considering whether there are ways of adapting it to provide what you want. If your house is too big, you might think about reusing the space in a better way. Would it be possible, for example, to turn a bedroom into a small upstairs study? Or perhaps you could convert a spare room into a separate workroom for hobbies and get rid of the clutter from the main living area? Have you thought about letting one or two rooms? As well as solving the problem of wasted space, it would also bring in some extra income.

Before embarking on any improvements, it is sensible to work out which ones will add the most value to your property. A loft conversion is a favourite as it can add an extra bedroom and possibly even a bathroom. Building an extra room as an extension is the next most popular – followed perhaps by adding a conservatory; a new kitchen and central heating; bathrooms and new windows.

A few judicious home improvements carried out now could make the world of difference in terms of comfort and practicality. Many of us carry on for years with inefficient heating systems that could be improved relatively easily and cheaply. Stairs need not necessarily be a problem, even when you are very much older, thanks to the many types of stair-lifts now available. Even so, a few basic facilities installed on the ground floor could save your legs in years to come. Similarly, gardens can be replanned to suit changing requirements; areas that now take hours to weed could be turned into extra lawn or a patio.

For some people, the problem is not so much the size or convenience of their home as the fact that they are unable to buy the freehold or extend the lease. They fear for their long-term security. But since the 1993 Leasehold Reform – Housing and Urban Development Act extended the right of enfranchisement to thousands of flat leaseholders, they now have the collective right to buy the freehold of their building and the individual right to extend their leases at a market price.

Among other requirements to enfranchise, your flat must be held under a lease that was originally granted for more than 21 years and the eligible tenants of at least half of the flats in the block must also wish to buy the freehold. Before proceeding, you would be advised to obtain a professional valuation as a first step to establishing a fair price to which the landlord would be entitled. 'Fair price' is made up of the open-market value of the building, half of any marriage value that may be payable plus possible compensation to the landlord for any severance or other losses. If you have a dwindling lease but do not wish to enfranchise, the more straightforward purchase of a 90-year lease extension might be a better option. For further information see leaflets: *Collective Enfranchisement – Getting started*; *Collective*

Enfranchisement – Valuation; *Lease Extension – Getting started* and *Lease Extension – Valuation*, obtainable free from LEASE at the address below.

If, as applies to many people, you want protection from a landlord but do not want to buy the freehold or extend your lease, you will be glad to know that leaseholders' rights have been strengthened over the last few years. Among other rights, where leaseholders believe that their service charges are unreasonable, they can ask a Leasehold Valuation Tribunal, rather than a court, to determine what charge is reasonable. This includes work that has been proposed but not yet started. Also, where there are serious problems with the management of a building, tenants can ask the Tribunal to appoint a new manager. Importantly, Leasehold Valuation Tribunals are less formal than a court and avoid the risk of potentially unknown costs being awarded, which can be the case with court proceedings. (Tribunals can award costs of up to £500 where they believe a person has acted abusively or otherwise unreasonably in connection with the proceedings.) For further information, obtain the booklet *Residential Long Leaseholders – Your rights and responsibilities*, available from Citizens Advice Bureaux or from the Department for Communities and Local Government Publications Centre: Tel: 0870 1226 236; e-mail: contactus@communities.gov.uk; website: www.communities.gov.uk.

Additionally, the Commonhold and Leasehold Reform Act 2002 introduces a new right to take over the management of flats without having to prove fault on the part of the landlord, makes buying the freehold or an extended lease of a flat easier, strengthens leaseholders' rights against unreasonable service charges, prevents landlords from taking any action for unpaid ground rent unless this has first been demanded in writing, makes lease variations easier to obtain and will also provide further protection for the holding of leaseholders' monies. Furthermore, landlords are not able to commence forfeiture proceedings to obtain possession of the property unless they have first proved an alleged breach of the lease before a Leasehold Valuation Tribunal. Where the breach relates to arrears, they must also have proved that the sum demanded is reasonable.

You could find it useful to ask LEASE for copies of their leaflets *The Right to Manage and Service Charges and Other Issues*. For general advice on leasehold, including lease-holders' rights and responsibilities, the contact number for the **Leasehold Advisory Service (LEASE)** is Tel: 020 7374 5380; e mail: info@lease-advice.org; website: www.leasc-advice.org. For advice on leasehold legislation and policy, get in touch with the **Department of Communities and Local Government, Leasehold & Park Homes Team,** contact: Tel: 020 7944 4287; website www.communities.gov.uk.

Moving to a new home

If you do decide to move, the sooner you start looking for your new home the better. There is no point in delaying the search until you retire and then rushing around expecting to find your dream house in a matter of weeks. With time to spare, you will have a far greater choice of properties and are less likely to indulge in any panic buying. Although a smaller house will almost certainly be easier and cheaper to

run, make sure that it is not so small that you are going to
feel cramped. Remember that when you and your partner
are both at home, you may need more room to avoid getting
on top of each other. Also, if your family lives in another
part of the country, you may wish to have them and your
grandchildren to stay. Conversely, beware of taking on
commitments such as a huge garden. Although this might be
a great source of enjoyment when you are in your 60s, it
could prove a burden as you become older.

If you are thinking of moving out of the neighbourhood,
there are other factors to be taken into account, such as
access to shops and social activities, proximity to friends and
relatives, availability of public transport and even health and
social support services. Although these may not seem particularly important now, they could become so in the future.
Couples who retire to a seemingly 'idyllic' spot often return
quite quickly. New friends are not always easy to make. So-
called 'retirement areas' can mean that you are cut off from
a normal cross-section of society and health services are
likely to be over-taxed. After a hard week's wheeling and
dealing it is tempting to wax lyrical about exchanging the
rat race for a life of rustic solitude. Although retiring to the
country can be glorious, city dwellers should, however, bear
in mind some of the less attractive sides of rural living.
Noise, for example low-flying aircraft and church bells, can
be an unexpected irritant. If you are not used to it, living
near a silage pit or farm can also be an unpleasant experience. Prices in village shops are often higher than in city
supermarkets and public transport tends to be infrequent.

Finally, would a small village or seaside resort offer sufficient scope to pursue your interests once the initial flurry of

activity is over? Even if you think you know an area well, check it out properly before coming to a final decision. If possible take a self-catering let for a couple of months, preferably out of season when rents are low and the weather is bad. A good idea is to limit your daily spending to your likely retirement income rather than splurge as most of us do on holiday. This is even more pertinent if you are thinking of moving abroad, where additional difficulties can include learning the language, lower standards of health care and the danger of losing contact with your friends. Another problem for expatriates could be a change in the political climate, resulting perhaps on the one hand in your not being so welcome in your adopted country and, on the other, in a drop in the purchasing power of your pension.

Counting the cost

Moving house can be an expensive exercise, but in the current economic climate, if you can afford to move, some good bargains can be had, as desirable purchasers are not too plentiful at present. It is estimated that the cost of moving is between 5 and 10 per cent of the value of a new home, once you have totted up such extras as search fees, removal charges, insurance, stamp duty, VAT, legal fees and estate agents' commission. Stamp duty applies to many properties costing over a certain price. Remember, the higher the price of the property, the more the stamp duty increases. If you plan any repairs, alterations or decorations, the figure will be considerably higher. On the other hand, if you move to smaller or cheaper accommodation you will be able to release money for other uses.

When buying a new home, especially an older property, it is essential to have a full building (structural) survey done before committing yourself. This will cost in the region of £500 for a small terraced house but is worth every penny. In particular, it will provide you with a come-back in law should things go wrong. A valuation report, although cheaper, is more superficial and may fail to detect flaws that could give you trouble and expense in the future.

If you are buying a newly built house, there are now a number of safeguards against defects. Most mortgagors will only lend on new homes with a National House Building Council (**NHBC**) warranty or its equivalent. The NHBC operates a 10-year **Buildmark** warranty and insurance scheme under which the builder is responsible for putting right defects during the first two years. It is designed to protect owners of newly built, or newly converted residential housing, if a problem does occur in a new home registered with NHBC. If the homeowner and builder do not agree on what needs to be done, NHBC can carry out a free independent resolution investigation and, if judged necessary, will instruct the builder to carry out repair works. If a problem becomes apparent after more than two years, the homeowner should contact NHBC, as the Buildmark covers a range of structural aspects as well as double-glazing, plastering and staircases. For more information, Tel: 0844 633 1000; e-mail: cssupport@nhbc.co.uk; website: www.nhbc.co.uk. Also helpful to home buyers, the Land Registry allows members of the public to seek information directly about the 20 million or so properties held on its register. The details can be accessed through Land Register Online or from one of its 24 local offices in England and Wales.

Alternatively contact the **Land Registry**: Tel: 0844 892 0456; website: www.landregisteronline.gov.uk.

Another welcome change is that conveyancing is now more competitive, with banks, building societies, insurance companies and other bodies (as well of course as solicitors) offering these services.

Home Information Packs: HIPs apply to residential properties marketed for sale. An HIP contains essential information concerning the property, including details of the terms of sale, title documents and deeds, local search information, any necessary warranties and the newly introduced Energy Performance Certificates. Costs vary from £300 to around £600. They are valid for as long as the property is continuously marketed for sale, and valid for up to one year where it is withdrawn from the market and re-marketed by the same owner. There is no requirement for any part of the HIP to be updated while the property is on the market. Four-bedroom plus properties required an HIP after 1 August 2007. Three-bedroom properties required an HIP if they were put on the market after 10 September 2007. Most other residential properties were required to have an HIP after 14 December 2007 whatever their size. There are certain exemptions. For full details and further information consult the Home Information Pack website: www.homeinformationpacks.gov.uk. Information on **Energy Performance Certificates** (EPCs) can be obtained via a helpline: Tel: 0845 365 2468; e-mail: help@epbduk.info; or the website: www.communities.gov.uk/epbd.

Bridging loans

Tempting as it may be to buy before you sell, unless you have the money available to finance the cost of two homes – including possibly two mortgages – you need to do your sums very carefully indeed. Bridging loans are a way of getting over the problem, but can be a very expensive option.

To give you an idea of the sorts of cost involved, banks usually charge 2 points or more over base rate plus an arrangement or administration fee on top. In other words, if bank rate is 5 per cent, the interest charged on a £100,000 loan works out at £583 a month: or £3,498 if it takes you six months to sell. Although by shopping around the building societies you may get somewhat better terms, you can easily work out that if your home is on the market for more than a very short while, the payments can escalate alarmingly. As an alternative to bridging loans, some of the major institutional estate agents operate chain-breaking schemes and may offer to buy your property at a discount: normally around 10 or 12 per cent less than the market price. In some circumstances this could be worthwhile, but as a lot of money is involved this is not a decision to be taken lightly.

Estate agents

Finding your dream home may prove harder than you think. The grapevine can be effective, so pass the word around about what you are looking for. The property advertisements, especially in local newspapers, may also be worth scanning. Additionally, you could contact a good estate agent in the area to which you want to move.

The **National Association of Estate Agents (NAEA)** runs a service called HomeLink, bringing together over 850 agency branches throughout Europe and the United Kingdom. Your nearest member of HomeLink can get details of houses for sale from a HomeLink member in your target area. For names of member agents, call the HomeLink Hotline: Tel: 01926 417792; e-mail: homelink@naea.co.uk; website: www.naea.co.uk.

Some building societies, banks and insurance companies – including Halifax and Legal & General – have created large chains of estate agents and many of these maintain systems for full exchange of information between their branches nationwide. All these, together with most other large groups as well as many independent estate agents, have introduced a Code of Practice and also formed an Ombudsman Scheme to provide an independent review service for buyers or sellers of UK residential property in the event of a complaint. The Ombudsman is empowered to make awards of up to £25,000. However, complaints must be reported to the company within 12 months of the incident and to the Ombudsman within six months of receiving the member agency's final letter. As with most ombudsman schemes, action can only be taken against firms that are actually members of the scheme. The Ombudsman also cannot intervene in disputes over surveys of the property. Copies of the *Consumer Guide*, the Code of Practice and other information can be obtained from member agencies or by contacting the Ombudsman direct. **The Ombudsman for Estate Agents**: Tel: 01722 333306; e-mail: admin@oea.co.uk; website: www.oea.co.uk.

A further welcome move to improve standards is the 1993 Property Misdescriptions Act, which prohibits estate agents and property developers from making misleading or inflated claims about a property, site or related matter. If you want to contact qualified local agents, **RICS (Royal Institution of Chartered Surveyors)** can provide names and addresses of chartered surveyors who are estate agents. Call their contact centre on Tel: 0870 333 1600; or e-mail: contactrics@rics. org; website: www.rics.org.

If you are thinking of retiring abroad, you must be careful not to be caught unawares by unscrupulous property developers. Many retired people wish to relocate to a warmer climate such as Mediterranean tourist resorts, but do not be rushed into a purchase you may later regret by fast-talking salespeople. Never make the mistake of putting down a deposit until you are as certain as you can be that you want to go ahead.

As well as all the obvious points such as water and electricity supply, it is essential to get the legal title and land rights thoroughly checked by an independent lawyer with specialist knowledge of the local property and planning laws. Otherwise you could be at risk of later discovering that the property you bought is not rightfully yours or, as recently happened to hundreds of homeowners in Spain, being informed that their home had been illegally built on greenbelt land and was due for demolition.

Removals

Transporting your worldly goods from A to B is an exhausting business. Professional help can remove many of the headaches if carried out by a reputable firm. Not only will they shift all the heavy furniture around for you, they will also wrap your china and ornaments safely in packing cases that they provide as part of the service. Costs vary depending on the type and size of furniture, the distance over which it is being moved and other factors, including insurance and seasonal troughs and peaks. Obviously, valuable antiques will cost more to pack and transport than standard modern furniture. It pays to shop around and get at least three written quotes from different removal firms. Some may be able to help reduce costs by arranging part or return loads. It is also worth asking whether the firm has a 'low-price day', as rates are often cheaper at the start of the week. Remember, however, that the cheapest quote is not necessarily the best. Find out exactly what you are paying for and whether the price includes packing and insurance.

A useful organisation to contact is the **British Association of Removers**. They will send you a free leaflet advising you what to do when you move house and a list of approved removal firms who all work to a rigorous Code of Practice. Tel: 01923 699 480; e-mail: info@bar.co.uk; website: www. bar.co.uk.

Retirement housing and sheltered accommodation

The terms 'retirement housing' and 'sheltered accommodation' cover a wide variety of housing but generally mean property with a resident manager/caretaker, an emergency alarm system, optional meals, and some communal facilities

such as living rooms, garden and laundry. Guest accommodation and visiting services such as hairdressers and
chiropodists are sometimes also available. A number of
companies offer extra care and nursing facilities in some of
their developments. Designed to bridge the gap between the
family home and residential care, such housing offers
continued independence for the fit and active within a secure
environment. Much of it is owned and run by local authorities, housing associations and charities. However, there are a
number of well-designed, high-quality private developments
of 'retirement homes' now on the market, for sale or rent, at
prices to suit most pockets.

Many of the more attractive properties – and among the
most expensive – are in converted country houses of archi-
tectural or historic merit or in newly developed 'villages' and
'courtyard' schemes. As a general rule, you have to be over
55 when you buy property of this kind. Although you may
not wish to move into this type of accommodation just now,
if the idea interests you in the long term it is worth planning
ahead as there are often very long waiting lists.

Other options

Boarding houses

At least 30,000 people live in privately run premises such as
boarding houses, guest houses, hotels or hostels, at which
they have accommodation, meals and some services, but not
nursing care. If you are attracted to this idea, make sure
you are dealing with a reputable establishment. Following

evidence that many retired people were being 'ripped off' by their landlords, anyone offering this type of accommodation to four or more people must now register with the local authority.

Caravan or mobile home

Many retired people consider living in a caravan or mobile home that they keep either in a relative's garden or on an established site, possibly at the seaside or in the country. You may already own one as a holiday home that you are thinking of turning into more permanent accommodation. If you want to live in a caravan on your own or other private land, you should contact your local authority for information about any planning permission or site licensing requirements that may apply.

If, on the other hand, you want to keep it on an established site, there is a varied choice ranging from small fields with just a handful of mobile homes to large, warden-assisted parks with shopping and leisure facilities. Make absolutely sure, whichever you choose, that the site owner has all the necessary permissions. You should check this with the planning and environmental health department of the local authority. It should be noted that many site owners will not accept prospective residents' own mobile homes, but require them to buy one from the site or from an outgoing resident. The rights of owners of residential mobile home sites and of residents who own their mobile home but rent their pitch from a site owner are set out in the Mobile Homes Act 1983.

Find out what conditions both the local authority and site owner attach to any agreement (by law the site owner must provide a written statement setting out such terms as the services provided, charges and maintenance of the site). You should also check your statutory rights (which should be included in the written statement), in particular regarding security of tenure and resale. Under the Act, residents have the right to sell their unit to a person approved by the site owner, who will be entitled to up to 10 per cent commission on the sale price. In the event of a dispute, either party is free to go to court or, with the agreement of both sides, to arbitration. If following a sale the resident is unhappy with the terms of the written agreement, appeal to the court must be within six months of the written terms being received.

It should also be noted that ordinary caravans are not always suitable as long-term accommodation for the over-60s. They can be damp as well as cramped, and what may have been an enjoyable adventure on holiday may soon pall when it is your only option. Modern residential-park homes, which are not all that different from bungalows, have the advantage of being more spacious and sturdier but, though usually cheaper than a house of equivalent size, are nevertheless a major expense. Moreover, the law regarding such purchases is complex and legal advice is very strongly recommended before entering into a commitment to purchase a park home.

Two companies that specialise in new homes for sale on residential parks, ready for immediate occupation are: **Britannia Parks:** Tel: 01252 408 891; website: www.britannia-parks.com, and **Omar Homes:** Tel: 01842 810673; website: www.omar.co.uk.

If you do decide to go ahead with the plan, you might like to obtain a copy of *Mobile Homes – A guide for residents and site owners*, a free booklet, available from your housing department or from the Department for Communities and Local Government: Tel: 0870 122 6236; e-mail: contactus@ communities.gov.uk; website: www.communities.gov.uk.

Self-build

Over 25,000 people a year, including many in their 50s, are now building their own homes and, with typical cost-savings estimated at between 25 and 40 per cent, the number has been growing. New building methods have been developed that defy the assumption that you need to be a fit young man to undertake such a project, and both women and elderly people have successfully become self-builders. No prior building experience is necessary, although this of course helps. Further good news is that in response to the demand some building societies offer self-build mortgages to enable borrowers to finance the purchase of land plus construction costs.

However, as with any mortgage, it is essential to make sure that you are not in danger of over-committing yourself. Not so long ago, hundreds of people lost their sites because, due to falling land prices, the size of their loan exceeded the value of the property – and by law building societies cannot make secured loans that are more than 100 per cent of the valuation.

It is also as well to be aware that obtaining planning permission from local councils can often be a protracted business and could add to the cost if you have to submit new plans. Most self-builders work in groups and/or employ sub-contractors for some of the more specialised work, but individuals who wish to build on their own can make arrangements with an architect or company that sells standard plans and building kits.

A useful organisation to contact is the **Walter Segal Self Build Trust**. This is a charitable trust, named after the architect who pioneered a practical post-and-beam timber-frame method of construction particularly appropriate for self-builders with no previous building skills. The Trust provides free advice and information on self-build methods, the costs involved and the financial options available. Website: www. segalselfbuild.co.uk; e-mail: geoff@segalselfbuild.co.uk.

Centre for Alternative Technology. The centre provides a free information and advice service on sustainable living and environmentally responsible building. Books on ecological building design and environmentally friendly products are available via mail order. Contact CAT by phone: Tel: 01654 705980; website: www.cat.org.uk.

2

Making your home more practical

It is sensible to set about any home improvement plans earlier rather than later. For one thing, these are often easier to afford when you are still earning a regular salary. For another, any building work is tiresome and most people find it easier to put up with the mess when they are not living among it 24 hours a day. Third, if you start early, you will enjoy the benefit that much sooner.

When embarking on changes a specific aim should be to make your home as economic, labour-saving and convenient as possible. Err on the side of simple systems rather than complex ones. You will be thankful you chose wisely as age increases. A reason for saying this is that many people become so involved with the add-ons or decorative aspects that they forget to think about some of the longer-term practicalities that, at next to no extra cost, could have been incorporated along with the other work.

Insulation

When you retire, you may be at home more during the day, so are likely to be using your heating more intensively. One of the best ways of reducing those now alarmingly increasingly costly utility bills is to get your house properly insulated. Heat escapes from a building in four main ways: through the roof, walls, floor and through loose-fitting doors and windows. Insulation not only cuts the heat loss dramatically but will usually more than pay for itself within four or five years.

Loft insulation. As much as 25 per cent of heat in a house escapes through the loft. The answer is to put a layer of insulating material, ideally 220 to 270 mm thick according to the material used, between and across the roof joists. You might be able to lay this yourself. The materials are readily available from builders' merchants. If you prefer to employ a specialist contractor, contact the **National Insulation Association** for a list of their members: Tel: 01525 383313; e-mail: info@nationalinsulationassociation.org.uk; website: www.nationalinsulationassociation.org.uk. Your local Age Concern group or volunteer bureau may also be able to help.

Doors and windows. A further 25 per cent of heat escapes through single-glazed windows, half of which could be saved through double-glazing. There are two main types: sealed units and secondary sashes (that can be removed in the summer). Compared with other forms of insulation, double glazing is expensive; however, it does have the advantage of reducing noise levels. As a result of new building regulations, which came into effect in April 2002, any replacement doors and windows installed after that date have to comply with strict thermal performance standards and the work will need to be done by an installer who is registered under the FENSA scheme. To be on the safe side, contact the **Glass and Glazing Federation**: Tel: 0870 042 4255; e-mail: info@ggf.org.uk; website: www.ggf.co.uk.

Effective draughtproofing saves heat loss as well as keeping out cold blasts of air. It is also relatively cheap and easy to install. Compression seals, mounted by a variety of methods and supplied in strip form, are the simplest and most cost-effective way to fill the gap between the fixed and moving edges of doors and windows. For draught-proofing older sliding sash windows and doors, wiper seals, fixed with rust-proof pins and screws, need to be used. For very loose-fitting frames, gap fillers that can be squeezed from a tube provide a more efficient seal between frame and surround, but this is normally work for a specialist. If you do fit draught seals, make sure you leave a space for a small amount of air to get through, or you may get problems with condensation. If the house is not well ventilated, you should put in a vapour check to slow down the leakage of moisture into the walls and ceiling. For advice on durable products and contractors, contact the **Draught Proofing Advisory Association**: Tel: 01428 654011; e-mail: dpaaassociation@aol.com; website: www.dpaa-association.org.uk.

Heat loss can also be considerably reduced through hanging heavy curtains (both lined and interlined) over windows and doors. Make sure all curtains cover the windowsill or rest on the floor. It is better to have them too long than too short.

Wall insulation. More heat is lost through the walls than perhaps anywhere else in the house: it can be as much as 50 per cent. If your house has cavity walls – and most houses built after 1930 do – then cavity wall insulation should be considered. This involves injecting mineral wool (rock wool or glass wool), polystyrene beads or foam into the cavity through holes drilled in the outside wall. It is work for a specialist and, depending on what grants are applicable, may be free or could cost upwards of £350. Against this, you could expect a typical saving of around 25 per cent off your heating bill each year, so that, in most cases, the initial outlay should be recovered in under four years. Make sure that the firm you use is registered with a reputable organisation, such as the British Standards Institution, or can show a current Agrément Certificate for the system and is approved by the BBA. If a foam fill is used, the application should comply with British Standard BS 5617 and the material with BS 5618.

Solid wall insulation can be considerably more expensive, but well worth while, providing similar savings of around 25 per cent off your annual heating bill. Again, this is work for a specialist and involves applying an insulating material to the outside of the wall, plus rendering or cladding. Alternatively, an insulated thermal lining can be applied to the inside. Landlords who install wall insulation can offset up to £1,500 of the cost, per building, against income tax.

nationalinsulationassociation.org.uk; website: www.nation
alinsulationassociation.org.uk.

Floor insulation. Up to 15 per cent of heat loss can be saved
through filling the cracks or gaps in the floorboards and
skirting. If you can take up your floorboards, rock wool or
glass wool rolls can be extremely effective when fixed under-
neath the joists. Filling spaces with papier mâché or plastic
wool will also help, especially if a good felt or rubber
underlay is then laid under the carpet. Be careful, however,
that you do not block up the underfloor ventilation, which is
necessary to protect floor timbers from dampness and rot.
Solid concrete floors can be covered with cork tiles or carpet
and felt or rubber underlay.

Hot-water cylinder insulation. If your hot-water cylinder
has no insulation, it could be costing you several pounds a
week in wasted heat. An insulating jacket around your hot-
water cylinder will cut wastage by three-quarters. Most
hot-water tanks now come ready supplied with insulation.
If not, the jacket should be at least 80 mm thick and will cost
from around £25. Jackets come in various sizes, so measure
your cylinder before buying and look for one that conforms
to BS 5615.

Grants

The government-funded Warm Front Grant scheme provides
grants up to £2,700 for home insulation and heating
measures and also gives energy efficiency advice. The grants
are mainly targeted at low-income householders – including
people who are disabled, chronically sick or over 60 – who

This used only to apply to loft and cavity wall insulatio⌐
has now been extended to include solid wall insulation.
scope of the relief (officially known as the Landlord's E⌐
Saving Allowance) was further extended to include dra⌐
proofing and insulation for hot-water systems. Since ⌐
2007, floor insulation is included in the list of energy-s⌐
items that quality for the allowance. NB: The £1,500
which previously applied to the building, now applie⌐
property. So if there are two flats in the building, the £1
cap now applies to each one.

For further information and addresses of registered con⌐
tors, contact:

British Board of Agrément: Tel: 01923 665300; e-⌐
contact@bba.star.co.uk; website: www.bbacerts.co.uk.

British Standards Institution: Tel: 020 8996 9001; e-⌐
csservices@bsigroup.com; website: www.bsigroup.co.uk⌐

Cavity Insulation Guarantee Agency (CIGA): Tel: 01⌐
853300; e-mail: info@ciga.co.uk; website: www.ciga.co.⌐

Eurisol UK Ltd: Tel: 020 7935 8532; e-mail: info@euri⌐
com; website: www.eurisol.com.

Insulated Render & Cladding Association Ltd (for solid
defective walls): Tel: 01428 654011; e-mail: incaassociat⌐
@aol.com; website: www.inca-ltd.org.uk.

National Insulation Association for cavity wall and ⌐
insulation, draughtproofing and insulated thermal lini⌐
(applied internally): Tel: 01525 383313; e-mail: inf⌐

own or privately rent their home. For further information, contact **Eaga plc**: Tel: 0800 316 6007; e-mail: enquiry@ eaga.com; website: www.eaga.com.

It might also be worth enquiring at your local authority whether it provides any assistance with insulation, and if so, whether you would be likely to qualify for help. There are no guarantees, however, as any such grants – other than mandatory Disabled Facilities Grants (see page 37) – are at the discretion of local authorities. For further information, contact the environmental health or housing department.

NB. The Chancellor has announced grants of between £300 and £4,000 for pensioners installing insulation and central heating in their homes. Further details can be obtained from the government's website: www.direct.gov.uk; or www. warmfront.co.uk.

Heating

It may be possible to save money by using different fuels or by heating parts of your house through different systems. This could apply especially if some rooms are only occasionally used. Your local gas and electricity offices can advise on heating systems, running costs and energy conservation, as well as heating and hot-water appliances. In particular, you might usefully enquire about Economy 7 electricity that provides cheaper-rate supplies at night.

The **Solid Fuel Association** will also give free advice and information on all aspects of solid fuel heating, including appliances and installation. Telephone their helpline on Tel: 0845 601 4406; or e-mail: sfa@solidfuel.co.uk; website: www.solidfuel.co.uk.

You could consult the **Building Centre**. It has a very wide range of building products on display, with information officers on hand to give consumer guidance: Tel: 020 7692 4000; e-mail: jseebalack@buildingcentre.co.uk; website: www.buildingcentre.co.uk.

Shopping note. Many people get rushed into expensive purchases on the promise of cheaper energy bills. A point to remember when comparing, say, gas with electricity is that fuel prices are volatile and relative cost advantages are not always maintained. If you have an otherwise adequate system, it could be a false economy to exchange it for the sake of a small saving in current heating costs.

Buying and installing heating equipment. When buying equipment, check that it has been approved by the appropriate standards approvals board. For electrical equipment, the letters to look for are BEAB (British Electro-technicals Approvals Board) or CCA (CENELEC Certification Agreement), which is the European Union equivalent.

For gas appliances, look for the CE mark, which denotes that appliances meet the requirements of the Gas Appliance (Safety) Regulations Act 1995. Domestic solid fuel appliances should be approved by the Solid Fuel Appliances Approval Scheme (see sales literature).

When looking for contractors to install your equipment, an important point to note is that new government legislation has come into force placing tighter controls on the standard of electrical and other installation work in households across England and Wales. It is now a legal requirement for electricians as well as kitchen, bathroom and gas installers to comply with Part P of the Building Regulations. You would therefore be well advised to check that any contractor you propose using is enrolled with the relevant inspection council or is a member of the relevant trade association.

Electricians should be approved by the **NICEIC**. All approved contractors are covered for technical work by the NICEIC Complaints Procedure and Guarantee of Standards Scheme and undertake to work to British Standard 7671. Any substandard work must be put right at no extra cost to the consumer. Names and addresses of local approved contractors can be found in the NICEIC Roll of Approved Contractors obtainable from NICEIC: Tel: 0870 013 0382; e-mail: enquiries@niceic.com; website: www.niceic.org.uk.

An alternative source for finding a reputable electrician is the **Electrical Contractors' Association**. Their members, all of whom have to be qualified, work to national wiring regulations and a published ECA Code of Fair Trading. There is also a Work Bond, which guarantees that, in the event of a contractor becoming insolvent, the work will be completed by another approved electrician at the originally quoted price, subject to the conditions of the scheme. Tel: 020 7313 4800; e-mail: info@eca.co.uk; website: www.eca.co.uk.

Gas appliances should only be installed by a CORGI (Council for Registered Gas Installers) registered installer. Registration is now compulsory by law. As a further safeguard, all registered gas installers carry a CORGI ID card with their photo, types of gas work they are competent to do, their employer's trading title and the CORGI logo. After a gas appliance has been installed, you should receive a safety certificate from CORGI, proving that it has been installed by a professional. You should keep this safe, as you may need it should you want to sell your home in the future. To find a registered installer in your area, contact **Council for Registered Gas Installers**: Tel: 0800 915 0485; e-mail: enquiries@trustcorgi.com; website: www.trustcorgi.com.

Additionally, members of the Heating and Ventilating Contractors' Association can advise on all types of central heating. All domestic installation work done by member companies is covered by a free three-year guarantee. For further information contact the **Heating and Ventilating Contractors' Association**: Tel: 020 7313 4900; e-mail: contact@hvca.org.uk; website: www.hvca.org.uk.

Tips for reducing your energy bills

Energy can be saved in lots of small ways. Taken together, they could amount to quite a large cut in your heating bills. You may find some of the following ideas worth considering:

■ Set your central heating timer and thermostat to suit the weather. A saving of half an hour or one degree can be substantial. For example, reducing the temperature by 1 degree Centigrade could cut your heating bills by up to 10 per cent.

▨ A separate thermostat on your hot-water cylinder set at around 60 degrees Centigrade will enable you to keep hot water for taps at a lower temperature than for the heating system.

▨ If you run your hot water off an immersion heater, have a time-switch fitted attached to an Economy 7 meter so that the water is heated at the cheap rate overnight. An override switch will enable you to top up the heat during the day if necessary.

▨ Showers are more economical than baths as well as being easier to use when you become older.

▨ Reflective foil sheets put behind your radiators help to reduce heat loss through the walls.

▨ Switch off, or reduce, the heating in rooms not being used and close doors.

▨ Low-energy light bulbs can save several pounds a year.

▨ If you have an open fire, a vast amount of heat tends to be lost up the chimney. A wood-burning stove can help reduce heat loss as well as maximise the amount of heat you get from your wood or solid fuel in other ways. If you dislike the idea of losing the look of an open fire, there are now a number of appliances on the market that are open-fronted and fit flush with the fireplace opening. Contact your local office of the Solid Fuel Association for further information. If you decide to block up a fireplace, don't forget to fit an air vent to allow some ventilation.

■ Some small cooking appliances can save energy in comparison with a full-sized cooker. An electric casserole or slow cooker uses only a fraction more energy than a light bulb and is economical for single households. Similarly, an electric frying pan or multi-cooker can be a sensible alternative for people living on their own. Pressure cookers and microwave ovens can save fuel and time.

■ Regularly defrosting fridges and freezers reduces running costs.

■ Finally, it is a good idea to get in the habit of reading your electricity and gas meters regularly. This will help you keep track of likely bills. British Gas customers can call the meter reading line, at any time 24 hours a day, to give your up-to-date readings. You should have your meter reading and account reference number to hand when you ring. Tel: 0800 107 0257.

You might like to take advantage of one of the British Gas Payment options that allows customers to spread their gas or electricity payments over the year in fixed monthly or quarterly instalments, based on an estimate of their annual consumption. Estimates are periodically adjusted up or down, depending on actual meter readings. Price reductions are offered to customers paying by monthly direct debit. For further details, contact British Gas (see your gas or electricity bill for telephone number; website: www.british gas.co.uk). Many other suppliers have similar budget plans..

Also useful to know, British Gas has a specially trained team of energy efficiency advisers who provide free advice on how to save energy over the phone and can also arrange a free energy efficiency audit for your home. Tel: 0800 512 012; website: www.britishgas.co.uk.

Useful reading

Saving Energy Saves Money and other useful guides. British Gas publishes a number of guides describing their many services, including several specifically aimed at older, disabled or chronically sick customers. Information includes advice on safety checks, services for visually impaired people, energy saving tips and other practical help. Available free from British Gas: Tel: 0800 512 012; website: www. britishgas.co.uk.

A free factsheet, *Help With Heating*, is available from Age Concern: Tel: 0800 00 99 66; website: www.ageconcern. org.uk. A separate Scottish version is available.

Other useful addresses

OFGEM is the regulator for the gas and electricity industry. Its main functions from a consumer point of view are: to promote competition between suppliers, to regulate the monopoly parts of the industry by setting price controls and standards of service, and to encourage companies to develop easy-payment terms for vulnerable and elderly customers. **OFGEM England**: Tel: 020 7901 7000. **OFGEM Scotland**: Tel: 0141 331 2678; e-mail: consumeraffairs@ofgem.gov.uk; website: www.ofgem.gov.uk.

Energywatch. This is the statutory body representing gas and electricity consumers' interests in England, Scotland and Wales. If you have a query or problem about your gas or electricity that you cannot resolve with the supplier, telephone Tel: 0845 906 0708; website: www.energywatch.org. uk.

Improvement and repair

Building work is notoriously expensive and can be a major deterrent to doing some of the alterations to your home that may be necessary. Before abandoning the idea, it is worth investigating whether you could take advantage of any assistance on offer. A bank loan may be the simplest way of raising funds for most repairs and improvements. Many banks and building societies are prepared to offer interest-only mortgages to older people to cover essential repairs and improvements.

If you are unlucky enough to discover dry rot or similar in your home, there is little you can do but try to ensure that the builder you employ does not do a botched job. Unfortunately, insurance cover does not usually extend to damage to your house caused by normal wear and tear, woodworm, rot, insects and vermin. If your house does need structural repairs, contact the Royal Institution of Chartered Surveyors (see 'Useful addresses', page 40). They will be able to advise you on your legal position as well as point you in the direction of reputable chartered surveyors.

Local authority assistance

The Regulatory Reform Order (RRO), which became law in 2002, gives local authorities greater discretionary powers to provide assistance – such as low-cost loans and grants – to help with renovations, repairs and adaptations to the home, or to help someone move to more suitable accommodation if that is a better solution. The RRO replaces the previous legislation governing renovation grant, common parts grant, HMO grant and home repair assistance and allows local authorities greater flexibility to determine their particular eligibility criteria, whether means testing should be involved and the actual type of assistance available. Any assistance given, however, must be in accordance with the authority's published policy. For further information contact the environmental health or housing department of your local authority.

Disabled Facilities Grant (DFG). This is designed to adapt or provide facilities for a home (including the common parts where applicable) to make it more suitable for occupation by a disabled person. It can cover a wide range of improvements to enable someone with a disability to manage more independently, including, for example, adaptations to make the accommodation safe for a disabled occupant, work to facilitate access either to the property itself or to the main rooms, the provision of suitable bathroom or kitchen facilities, the adaptation of heating or lighting controls, or improvement of the heating system. Provided the applicant is eligible, a mandatory grant of up to £25,000 may be available in England for all the above (local authorities may use their discretionary powers to provide additional assistance).

As with most other grants, there is a means test. The local authority will want to check that the proposed work is reasonable and practicable according to the age/condition of the property and the local social services department will need to be satisfied that the work is necessary and appropriate to meet the individual's needs. The grant can be applied for either by the disabled person or by a joint owner/tenant or landlord on his/her behalf. For further information, contact the environmental health or housing department of your local authority. See also the leaflet *Disabled Facilities Grant*, obtainable from DCLG Free Literature: Tel: 0870 122 6236; e-mail: contactus@communities.gov.uk; website: www.communities.gov.uk.

Do not start work until approval has been given to your grant application, as you will not be eligible for a grant once work has started.

Community care grant. Income support recipients may be able to obtain a community care grant from the Social Fund to help with repairs. For further information, see leaflet GL18 *Help from the Social Fund*, obtainable from any social security office.

Other help for disabled people. Your local authority may be able to help with the provision of certain special facilities such as a stairlift, telephone installations or a ramp to replace steps. Apply to your local social services department, and if you encounter any difficulties, ask for further help from your local Disability Group or Age Concern Group.

Useful addresses

APHC Ltd (Association of Plumbing & Heating Contractors Ltd) maintains a national register of licensed members and can put you in touch with a reputable local engineer. All are carefully vetted every year to ensure they are working to the highest standards. Tel: 024 7647 0626; e-mail: switchboard@competentpersonscheme.co.uk; website: www.com petentpersonsscheme.co.uk.

Association of Building Engineers can supply names of qualified building engineers/surveyors: Tel: 0845 126 1058; e-mail: building.engineers@abe.org.uk; website: www.abe. org.uk.

Association of Master Upholsterers & Soft Furnishers Ltd has a list of over 500 approved members throughout the country who specialise in all forms of upholstery, including curtains and soft furnishings. Names of those operating in your area can be obtained from them: Tel: 029 2077 8918; website: www.upholsterers.co.uk.

The Building Centre has displays of building products, heating appliances, bathroom and kitchen equipment and other exhibits and can give guidance on building problems. It has manufacturers' lists and other free literature that you can take away and there is also a well-stocked bookshop covering all aspects of building and home improvement. Open Monday to Friday, 9.30 am to 6 pm; Saturday, 10 am to 2 pm. Tel: 020 7692 4000; website: www.buildingcentre. co.uk.

Federation of Master Builders (FMB) lists of members are available from regional offices. A warranty scheme, which insures work in progress and gives up to 10 years' guarantee on completion of work, is available from some of its members. Tel: 020 7242 7583; website: www.fmb.org.uk.

Guild of Master Craftsmen can supply names of all types of specialist craftspeople including, for example, carpenters, joiners, ceramic workers and restorers. Tel: 01273 478449; e-mail: theguild@thegmcgroup.com; website: www.guildmc.com.

Institute of Plumbing and Heating Engineering can provide a list of professional plumbers. Tel: 01708 472791; e-mail: info@ciphe.org.uk; website: www.iphe.org.uk.

Property Care Association has remedial treatment companies throughout the United Kingdom and can recommend reputable damp-proofing companies in your area as well as independent consultants, freelance surveyors and members specialising in cellar basement conversions. Tel: 0870 121 6737; e-mail: pca@property-care.org; website: www.property-care.org.

Royal Institute of British Architects (RIBA) has a free Clients' Service, which, however small your building project, will recommend up to three suitable architects. It can also supply you with useful leaflets giving advice on working with an architect. Tel: 020 7580 5533; e-mail: info@inst.riba.org; website: www.architecture.com.

RICS (Royal Institution of Chartered Surveyors) will nominate qualified surveyors in your area who can be recognised by the initials MRICS or FRICS after their name. It also publishes a number of useful leaflets. Tel: 0870 333 1600; e-mail: contactrics@rics.org; website: www.rics.org.

The Scottish and Northern Ireland Plumbing Employers' Federation (SNIPEF) is the national trade association for all types of firms involved in plumbing and domestic heating in Scotland and Northern Ireland. It has over 800 member firms and operates a code of fair trading, independent complaints scheme and guarantee of work scheme. Lists of local members are available on request. Tel: 0131 225 2255; e-mail: info@snipef.org; website: www.snipef. org.

Useful reading

Older Home Owners – Financial help with repairs and adaptations, free factsheet, is available from Age Concern: Tel: 0800 00 99 66; website: www.ageconcern.org.uk. A separate Scottish version is available.

Home improvement agencies (HIAs)

Home Improvement Agencies (sometimes known as 'staying put' or 'care and repair' agencies) work with older or disabled people to help them remain in their own homes by providing advice and assistance on repairs, improvements and adaptations. They also advise on the availability of funding and welfare benefits, obtain prices, recommend reliable builders and inspect the completed job.

For information about your nearest HIA, contact **Foundations**: Tel: 01457 891909; email: foundations@ cel.co.uk. You can search the website for a directory of local Home Improvement Agencies: website: www.foundations. uk.com. Your local authority or Citizens Advice Bureau will also know about local schemes.

Another possibility is to contact Anchor Trust, which has 'staying put' agencies across England. **Anchor Staying Put**: Tel: 0191 270 6069; e-mail: ann.young@anchor.org.uk; website: www.stayingput.org.uk.

3

Safety in the home

Accidents in the home account for 40 per cent of all fatal accidents, resulting in nearly 5,000 deaths a year. Seventy per cent of these victims are over retirement age and nearly 80 per cent of deaths are caused by falls. A further three million people need medical treatment. The vast majority of accidents are caused by carelessness or by obvious danger spots in the home that for the most part could very easily be made safer. Tragically, it is all too often the little things that we keep meaning to attend to but never quite get round to that are the ones that prove fatal.

Steps and stairs should be well lit, with light switches at both the top and bottom. Frayed carpet is notoriously easy to trip on. On staircases especially, carpet should be repaired or replaced as soon as possible. All stairs should have a handrail along the wall to provide extra support – on both sides, if the stairs are very steep. It is also a good idea to have a white line painted on the edge of steps that are difficult to see – for instance in the garden or leading up to the front door.

It may be stating the obvious to say that climbing on chairs and tables is dangerous – and yet we all do this. You should keep proper steps, preferably with a handrail, to do high jobs in the house such as hanging curtains or reaching top cupboards.

Floors can be another danger zone. Rugs and mats can slip on polished floors and should always be laid on some form of non-slip backing material. Stockinged feet are slippery on all but carpeted floors and new shoes should always have the soles scratched before you wear them. Remember also that spilt water or talcum powder on tiled or linoleum floors is a number one cause of accidents.

The **bathroom** is particularly hazardous for falls. Sensible precautionary measures include using a suction-type bath mat and putting handrails on the bath or alongside the shower. For older people who have difficulty getting in and out of the bath, a bath seat can be helpful. Soap on a rope is safer in a shower, as it is less likely to slither out of your hands and make the floor slippery. Regardless of age, you should make sure that all medicines are clearly labelled. Throw away any prescribed drugs left over from a previous illness.

Fires can all too easily start in the home. If you have an open fire, you should always use a fireguard and sparkguard at night. The chimney should be regularly swept, at least once a year, maybe more if you have a wood-burning stove. Never place a clotheshorse near an open fire or heater, and be careful of inflammable objects that could fall from the mantelpiece. Upholstered furniture is a particular fire hazard, especially when polyurethane foam has been used in its manufacture. If buying new furniture, make sure that it carries a red triangle label, indicating that it is resistant to smouldering cigarettes. Furniture that also passes the match ignition test carries a green label. Since March 1989, the use of polyurethane foam in furniture manufacture has been banned and 'combustion modified foam' which has passed the BS 5852 test now has to be used instead.

Portable heaters should be kept away from furniture and curtains and positioned where you cannot trip over them. Paraffin heaters should be handled particularly carefully and should never be filled while alight. Avoid leaving paraffin where it will be exposed to heat, including sunlight. If possible, it should be kept in a metal container outside the house.

Gas appliances should be serviced regularly by British Gas or another CORGI-registered installer. You should also ensure that there is adequate ventilation when using heaters. Never block up air vents: carbon monoxide fumes can kill.

British Gas publishes a free leaflet on *The Dangers of Carbon Monoxide Poisoning*, which includes advice on how to recognise danger signs as well as how to use your gas appliances safely and effectively. A free safety check on gas appliances is available to any British Gas customer living alone who is over the age of 60 or registered disabled or chronically sick. It is also available to customers living with other people where everyone, like themselves, is either over 60, registered disabled or chronically sick. Those wishing to use the service will first need to ring British Gas to be listed on their Home EnergyCare Register on Tel: 0800 33 66 99.

If you smell gas or notice anything you suspect could be dangerous, stop using the appliance immediately, open the doors and windows and call the **National Grid** (formerly Transco) 24 hour emergency line free on Tel: 0800 111 999.

More than one in three fires in the home are caused by accidents with **cookers**. Chip pans are a particular hazard: only fill the pan one-third full with oil and always dry the chips before putting them in the fat. Or better still, use oven-ready chips that you just pop into the oven to cook. Pan handles should be turned away from the heat and positioned so you cannot knock them off the stove. If called to the door or telephone, always take the pan off the ring and turn off the heat before you leave the kitchen. Cigarettes left smouldering in an ashtray could be dangerous if the ashtray is full. Smoking in bed is a potential killer!

Faulty electric wiring is another frequent cause of fires, as are overloaded power points. The wiring in your home should be checked every five years and you should avoid using too many appliances off a single plug. Ask an electrician's advice about what is the maximum safe number. Only use plugs that conform to the British Standard 1363. It is a good idea to get into the habit of pulling the plug out of the wall socket when you have finished using an appliance, whether TV or toaster.

All electrical equipment should be regularly checked for wear and tear, and frayed or damaged flexes immediately replaced. Wherever possible, have electric sockets moved to waist height to avoid unnecessary bending whenever you want to turn on the switch. In particular, **electric blankets** should be routinely overhauled and checked in accordance with the manufacturer's instructions. It is dangerous to use both a hot water bottle and an electric blanket – and never use an underblanket as an overblanket.

Electrical appliances are an increasing feature of labour-saving **gardening** but can be dangerous unless treated with respect. They should never be used when it is raining. Moreover, gardeners should always wear rubber-soled shoes or boots, and avoid floppy clothing that could get caught in the equipment.

As a general precaution, keep **fire extinguishers** readily accessible. Make sure they are regularly maintained and in good working order. Portable extinguishers should conform to BS EN3 or BS 6165. Any extinguishers made before 1996 should conform to BS 5423, which preceded BS EN3. Many insurance companies now recommend that you install a smoke alarm, which should conform to BS 5446–1: 2000 or BS EN14604: 2005, as an effective and cheap early-warning device. Prices from about £10.

Useful reading

Your Safety, *Fire*, *Keep Out the Cold* and *Your Security*, free from the Information Resources Team, Help the Aged: Tel: 020 7278 1114; e-mail: info@helptheaged.org.uk; website: www.helptheaged.org.uk.

Home security

Nine out of 10 burglaries are spontaneous and take less than 10 minutes. However, there is much you can do to protect yourself. The crime prevention officer at your local police station will advise you how to improve your security arrangements. He will also tell you whether there is a Neighbourhood Watch Scheme and how you join it. This is a free service that the police are happy to provide.

The most vulnerable access points are doors and windows. Simple precautions such as fitting adequate locks and bolts can do much to deter the average burglar. Prices for a good door lock are about £60 to £80 plus VAT, and prices for window locks about £15 to £20 plus VAT per window. Doors should have secure bolts or a five-lever mortise lock strengthened by metal plates on both sides, a door chain and a spyhole in the front door. Additionally, you might consider outside lights (ideally with infrared sensor) to illuminate night-time visitors and an entry-phone system requiring callers to identify themselves before you open the door.

Windows should also be properly secured with key-operated locks. Best advice is to fit locks to secure them when partially open. Install rack bolts or surface-mounted security pressbolts on french windows and draw your curtains at night, so potential intruders cannot see in. Louvre windows are especially vulnerable because the slats can easily be removed. A solution is to glue them in place with an epoxy resin and to fit a special louvre lock. An agile thief can get through any space larger than a human head, so even small windows such as skylights need properly fitted locks. Both double-glazing and venetian blinds act as a further deterrent.

If you are particularly worried, you could also have bars fitted to the windows or install old-fashioned internal shutters that can be closed at night. Alternatively, many DIY shops sell decorative wrought-iron security grilles.

An obvious point is to ensure that the house is securely locked whenever you go out, even for five minutes. If you lose your keys, you should change the locks without delay. Insist that official callers such as meter readers show their identity cards before you allow them inside. If you are going away, even for only a couple of days, remember to cancel the milk and the newspapers. You may also like to take advantage of the Royal Mail's **Keepsafe** service. It will store your mail while you are away and so avoid it piling up and alerting potential burglars to your absence. There is a charge for the service, which varies from £5.70 for up to 17 days to £17.15 for 66 days; a week's notice is necessary. Application forms are obtainable from the Post Office or by calling the Royal Mail Enquiry Line on Tel: 08457 777 888; website: www.royalmail.com.

If your home will be unoccupied for any length of time, it would be sensible to ask the local police to put it on their unattended premises register. Finally, consider a time switch (cost around £15), which will turn the lights on and off when you are away and can be used to switch on the heating before your return.

If you want to know of a reputable locksmith, you should contact the **Master Locksmiths Association**, which can either give you the name of an approved locksmith in your area over the telephone or send you a list of their members, classified county by county. Tel: 01327 262 255; e-mail:

enquiries@locksmiths.co.uk; website: www.locksmiths.co.
uk.

The Home Office issues a couple of useful booklets, *Your
Practical Guide to Crime Prevention* and *How to Beat the
Bogus Caller*. Available free from your local police station,
or telephone Tel: 0870 241 4680.

Burglar alarms and safes

More elaborate precautions such as a burglar alarm are one
of the best ways of protecting your home. Although expensive – alarms cost from about £450 to well in excess of
£1,000 for sophisticated systems – they could be worth
every penny. In the event of a break-in, you can summon
help or ask the police to do what they can if you are away.

Many insurance companies will recommend suitable
contractors to install burglar alarm equipment. Alternatively, contact **National Security Inspectorate** who will
send a free list of approved contractors in your locality who
install burglar alarm systems to, among other, British and
European Standards – there are 700 recognised firms and
some 1,000 branches. The National Security Inspectorate
will also investigate technical complaints. Tel: 0845 006
3003; e-mail: nsi@nsi.org.uk; website: www.nsi.org.uk.

If you keep valuables or money in the house, you should
think about buying a concealed wall or floor safe. If you are
going away, it is a good idea to inform your neighbours so
that if your alarm goes off they will know something is
wrong. Burglar alarms have an unfortunate habit of ringing

for no reason (a mouse or cat can trigger the mechanism), and many people ignore them as a result. It is advisable to give your neighbours a key so that they can turn off and reset the alarm should the occasion arise.

Insurance discounts

According to recent research, seven out of 10 householders are under-insured, some of them unknowingly but some intentionally to keep premiums lower. This could be dangerous because in the event of a mishap they could end up seriously out of pocket. With recent increases in premiums, many readers may feel that this is hardly the moment to be discussing any reassessment of their policy. However, there are two good reasons why this could be sensible: first, because the number of burglaries has risen, so the risks are greater; second, because you may be able to obtain better value than you are getting at present. As you may know, a number of insurance companies now give discounts on house contents premiums if proper security precautions have been installed. These include Cornhill Direct, Royal & Sun Alliance and Direct Line.

Some insurance companies approach the problem differently and arrange discounts for their policyholders with manufacturers of security devices. If you would welcome independent advice on choosing a policy, you might usefully contact the **Institute of Insurance Brokers** for details of local IIB brokers: Tel: 01933 410003; e-mail: inst.ins.brokers@iib-uk.com; website: www.iib-uk.com. See also section headed 'Insurance', page 53.

Personal safety

Older people who live on their own can be particularly at risk. A number of personal alarms are now available that are highly effective and can generally ease your peace of mind. A sensible precaution is to carry a 'screamer alarm', sometimes known as a 'personal attack button'. These are readily available in department stores, electrical shops and alarm companies.

Age Concern Aid-Call provides a service that enables anyone living alone to call for help simply by pressing a button. The subscriber has a small radio transmitter, worn as a pendant or like a watch, that contacts a 24-hour monitoring centre. The centre alerts a list of nominated relatives and friends, or the emergency services, that something is wrong. There are several ways of paying for Aid-Call based on installation, monitoring and rental. The firm operates a nationwide service and will arrange a demonstration through its head office. For a brochure, contact **Age Concern Aid-Call**: Tel: 0800 77 22 66; e-mail: info@aidcall-alarms.co.uk; website: www.aidcall.co.uk.

A telephone can also increase your sense of security. Some families come to an arrangement whereby they ring their older relatives at regular times to check that all is well. Older people feel particularly vulnerable to mugging. Although the dangers are often exaggerated, it must be sensible to take all normal precautions. The police are of the view that many muggings could be avoided if you are alert, think ahead and try to radiate confidence.

Insurance

As you near retirement, it is sensible to reassess your building and home contents policy. If the insurance was originally arranged through your building society it may cease when your mortgage is paid off. In this case it will be essential for you to arrange new cover directly. Similarly, when buying for cash – for instance when moving to a smaller house – it will be up to you to organise the insurance and to calculate the rebuilding value of your home. It is advisable to get a qualified valuer to do this for you.

Home values have increased dramatically over the last 15 years, and although values are now lower than they were, the chances are that the cost of replacing the fabric of your house, were it to burn down, would be significantly greater than the amount for which it is currently insured. Remember, you must insure for the full rebuilding cost: market value may be inadequate. Your policy should also provide money to meet architects' or surveyors' fees, as well as alternative accommodation for you and your family if your home were completely destroyed.

If you are planning to move into accommodation that has been converted from one large house into several flats or maisonettes, check with the landlord or managing agent that the insurance on the structure of the total building is adequate. All too many people have found themselves homeless because each tenant only insured his or her own flat and the collective policies were not sufficient to replace the common parts.

If when buying a new property you decide to take out a new mortgage, contrary to what many people believe you are under no obligation to insure your home with the particular company suggested by your building society. It is not being recommended here that you should necessarily go elsewhere. The point is that, as with all insurance, policies vary and some are more competitive than others.

In 2007 many people were affected by some of the worst flooding for decades. About two million people live under threat of flooding in the United Kingdom – about one in ten homes – and over 270,000 properties are at risk. It is highly advisable to check whether you live in a high-risk area and if so take steps to protect your property. This could cut your insurance premium by 10 per cent. According to the Association of British Insurers it can cost up to £40,000 to fully protect your home from flood damage. Further information can be obtained by calling the Floodline on 0845 988 1188, or check the Environment Agency website: www.environment-agency.gov.uk.

Many people are woefully under-insured with regard to the contents of their home. Insurance that simply covers the purchase price is normally grossly insufficient. Instead, you should assess the replacement cost and make sure you have a 'new for old' or 'replacement as new' policy. Most insurance companies offer an automatic inflation-proofing option for both building and contents policies. Although it is obviously prudent to take advantage of this, many people unthinkingly sign on the dotted line, quite forgetting to cancel items such as furniture or jewellery that they may have given away or sold – and so are encumbered with higher charges than necessary. Equally, many forget to add new valuables they have bought or received as presents. In particular, do check that you are adequately covered for any home improvements you may have undertaken such as an American-style kitchen, new garage, conservatory, extra bathroom, swimming pool or other luxury.

Where antiques and jewellery are concerned, simple inflation-proofing may not be enough. Values can rise and fall disproportionately to inflation and depend on current market trends. For a professional valuation, contact either the **British Antique Dealers' Association (BADA)**: Tel: 020 7589 4128; website: www.bada.org; or **LAPADA (the Association of Art & Antiques Dealers)**: Tel: 020 7823 3511; website: www.lapada.org, for the name of a specialist. Photographs of particularly valuable antiques can help in the assessment of premiums and settlement of claims as well as give the police a greater chance of recovering the items in the case of theft. Property marking, for example with an ultraviolet marker, is another useful ploy as it will help the police trace your possessions should any be stolen.

The **Association of British Insurers** will send you information sheets on various aspects of household insurance and loss prevention, including *Buildings Insurance for Home Owners* and *Home Contents Insurance*, which describe what policies you need and advise on how to ensure you have the correct amount of cover. Tel: 020 7600 3333; e-mail: info@abi.org.uk; website: www.abi.org.uk.

The **British Insurance Brokers' Association** can provide you with a list of registered insurance brokers in your area. Contact Consumers' Helpline: Tel: 0870 950 1790; e-mail: enquiries@biba.org.uk; website: www.biba.org.uk.

Some insurance companies offer home and contents policies for older people (age 50 and over) at substantially reduced rates. The rationale behind such schemes is that older people are less likely to leave their homes empty on a regular basis (eg 9 to 5) and are therefore less liable to be burgled. In some cases also, policies are geared to the fact that many retired people have either sold or given away many of their more valuable possessions and therefore only need to insure their homes up to a relatively low sum.

Such policies are arranged through **Age Concern Insurance Services**: Tel: 0800 169 2700; website: www.ageconcern. org.uk; **Saga Services Ltd**: Tel: 0800 068 8412; website: www.saga.co.uk; and **Help the Aged Insurance**: Tel: 0800 413180; website: www.helptheaged.org.uk.

An increasing number of insurance companies, including Legal & General, offer generous no claims discounts. Another type of discount-linked policy that is becoming more popular is one that carries an excess, whereby the householder pays the first chunk of any claim – say, the first £100 or £250. Savings on premiums can be quite appreciable, so it is certainly worth asking your insurance company what terms they offer. If these are not very attractive, it could pay you to shop around for a better deal.

4

Raising money on your home

The problem for many retired people is that they are 'asset rich, cash poor', with their main asset being their home. As a result, many retired owner-occupiers have substantial amounts of money tied up in their homes while they struggle to make ends meet on reduced incomes. One way round the dilemma is to sell up and move somewhere smaller in order to provide extra income. For those who prefer to stay put, however, there are a number of schemes that enable people to unlock capital without having to move. Generally known as equity release plans, these usually fall into one of three categories: reversion schemes, lifetime mortgages and home income plans. Although all have their attractions, no such scheme is without its drawbacks, so it is essential to make sure that you fully understand all the financial implications – including how the plan might affect your estate – before entering into any agreement.

A crucial point to check is that any plan you are considering carries an absolute guarantee of your being able to remain in your home for as long as you need or want to do so. In the past, many elderly people tragically lost their homes as a result of ill-advised and dangerous schemes. Today it is extremely unlikely that you would be offered a high-risk plan because in October 2004 all lifetime mortgages and home income plans came under the regulation of the FSA. But where your home is concerned you simply cannot afford to take any chances. Since April 2007, reversion schemes have also come under the regulation of the FSA.

In a welcome move to establish best practice and to give individuals greater protection, 21 leading providers – Bradford & Bingley, Bridgewater Equity Release Ltd, Bristol & West Plc, Coventry Building Society, Dunfermline Building Society, Hodge Equity Release, Home & Capital, In Retirement Services, Just Retirement, LV=, More2Life, National Counties Building Society, New Life Mortgages Ltd, Northern Rock Plc, Norwich Union Equity Release Ltd, Partnership Home Loans Ltd, Prudential, Retirement Plus Ltd, Standard Life Bank Freestyle Lifetime Mortgages Ltd, Stonehaven, Stroud & Swindon Building Society – have become a self-regulatory group, known as **SHIP (Safe Home Income Plans)**. All abide by a code of conduct and undertake to give a full and fair presentation of any plan offered, including what costs are involved and how the plan would affect the value of the person's estate. As a further safeguard, they will not finalise an arrangement without a certificate signed by the applicant's solicitor, confirming that they have fully explained the terms of the contract to their client.

SHIP advises that before signing anything, you seek clarification on any of the following points that are not already crystal clear:

- how the value of your estate would be affected;

- what this could mean in terms of loss to your heirs;

- whether the value of any plan benefits could be eroded by inflation;

- how the rise or fall in property prices could affect you;

- the setting-up costs and/or other arrangement charges;

- whether your state of health affects the plan in any way;

- the position should you want to move;

- whether the extra money would make sufficient difference to justify proceeding with the scheme.

Though not essential, SHIP suggests that before finally committing yourself, it could be sensible to discuss the idea with close family. **SHIP Safe Home Income Plans**: Tel: 0870 241 6060; e-mail: info@ship-ltd.org; website: www.ship-ltd.

One organisation it may be worth considering is **Houseproud**, which offers access to empathetic, low set-up cost, equity release for sums from as little as £3,000. Lenders are

FSA regulated and the equity release comes with a guarantee of no repossession and no negative equity. For further information, contact: Tel: 0115 934 9508; e-mail: info@hittrust. org; website: www.houseproud.org.uk.

Home reversion schemes

Home reversion schemes work as follows. You sell the ownership of all or part of your home to the reversion company for an agreed sum of money, and additionally retain the right to live in the property for the rest of your life or until the plan comes to an end due to the need for long-term care. You will not be charged any interest payments and normally the setting-up costs are fairly low. However, the downside is that the money you receive from the sale will be substantially less than the current market value of your home. The price paid will reflect the fact that it could be a great many years before the reversion company can realise its investment. The longer you live, the more value you will get from the scheme. If your life expectancy is not that great, a particular point to query is whether there are any benefit guarantees in the event of early death. Home reversion plans are offered by:

Bridgewater Equity Release Ltd. Tel: 0808 100 1065; website: www.bridgewaterequityrelease.co.uk.

Hodge Equity Release. Tel: 0800 731 4076; website: www.HodgeEquityRelease.com.

Home & Capital. Tel: 0800 253 657; website: www.home-capital.co.uk.

In Retirement Services. Tel: 0800 70 75 80; website: www.inretirementservices.co.uk.

Key Retirement Solutions. Tel: 0800 531 6027; website: www.keyrs.co.uk.

LV=. Tel: 0870 609 0616; website: www.LV.com.

Norwich Union Equity Release. Tel: 0845 302 0111; website: www.norwichunion.com.

Partnership Home Loans. Tel: 0845 108 7240; website: www.partnershiphomeloans.co.uk.

Retirement Plus Ltd. Tel: 0845 850 8510; website: www.retirement-plus.co.uk.

Lifetime mortgages

Lifetime mortgages (sometimes known as roll-up loans) advance you a sum of money, or regular income or an initial sum plus drawdown facility, on which you pay no interest during your lifetime. Instead, the interest payments are added to the original loan at compound rates and are repaid from your estate on death. Although attractive in that recipients can spend the money safe in the knowledge that they will not have to make any repayments, the disadvantage is that compound interest can very quickly mount up, leaving little or nothing for their heirs to inherit. To reduce the risk, particular points to check are, first, that the interest is fixed rather than variable and, even more important, that the plan includes a guarantee (as all SHIP company plans do) that there is no danger to your estate of negative equity. Roll-up loans are offered by:

Bradford & Bingley. Tel: 0800 11 33 33; website: www.bradfordandbingley.co.uk.

Bristol & West Mortgages. Tel: 0845 300 8000; website: www.bristolandwest4brokers.co.uk.

Hodge Equity Release. Tel: 0800 731 4076; website: www.HodgeEquityRelease.com.

Just Retirement Ltd. Tel: 01737 233296; website: www.justretirement.com.

LV=. Tel: 0870 609 0616; website: www.LV.com.

New Life Mortgages Ltd. Tel: 0121 712 3800; website: www.newlifemortgages.co.uk.

Northern Rock Plc. Tel: 0845 60 50 500; website: www.northernrock.com.

Norwich Union Equity Release Ltd. Tel: 0845 302 0111; website: www.norwichunion.com.

Prudential. Tel: 0800 316 9959; website: www.pru.co.uk.

Standard Life Lifetime Mortgage. Tel: 0845 609 0254; website: www.freestylemortgages.com.

Home income plans

Home income plans work on the basis of a mortgage arrangement whereby the loan is used to purchase an annuity to provide a guaranteed income for life. The mortgage interest is fixed and is deducted from the annuity payment before you receive your share. Although popular at one time, such plans have largely fallen out of favour due to the abolition of mortgage interest relief and worsening annuity rates. They are still available, but the view from SHIP is that few people would derive much value and that they should really only be considered by those well into their mid-80s. Home income plans are offered by the following companies:

Hodge Equity Release. Tel: 0800 731 4076; website: www.HodgeEquityRelease.com.

LV=. Tel: 0870 609 0616; website: www.LV.com.

Cashing in on the value of your home, while continuing to live there for the remainder of your life, has attractive advantages, especially if the priority is to generate additional income or to provide you with a lump sum. However, despite the new regulatory requirement and the existence of SHIP with its stringent code of conduct, expert advice is essential. SHIP recommends that in addition to a discussion with a solicitor – which is an obligatory condition of sale for all SHIP companies before finalising a plan on a client's behalf – you should also consult an independent financial adviser (IFA) with expertise in equity release schemes. A welcome safeguard is that the Financial Services Authority, which regulates lifetime mortgages, extended its powers to include home reversion schemes in April 2007.

For further information, contact specialist advisers **Hinton & Wild (Home Plans) Ltd**: Tel: 0800 328 8432; e-mail: info@hinton-wild.co.uk; website: www.hinton-wild.co.uk.

Useful reading

Extra Capital and Income for Older Home Owners; *Safe Home Income Plans*; and *Everything You Need to Know Before You Take Out a Plan*, free from Hinton & Wild (Home Plans) Ltd.

Using Your Home to Improve Your Finances, free guide from Age Concern: Tel: 0800 169 5276.

5

Using your home to earn money

Rather than move, many people whose home has become too large are tempted by the idea of taking in tenants. For some, it is an ideal plan; for others, a disaster. At best, it could provide you with extra income and the possibility of pleasant company. At worst, you could be involved in a lengthy legal battle to regain possession of your property. Before you either rush off to put a card in the newsagent's window or reject the idea out of hand, it is helpful to understand the different options, together with your various rights and responsibilities.

There are three broad choices: taking in paying guests or lodgers, letting part of your home as self-contained accommodation, or renting the whole house for a specified period of time. In all cases, for your own protection it is essential to have a written agreement and to take up bank references, unless the let is a strictly temporary one where the money is paid in advance. Otherwise, rent should be collected quarterly and you should arrange a hefty deposit to cover any damage. An important point to be aware of is that there is now a set of strict rules concerning the treatment of deposits, with the risk of large fines for landlords and agents who fail to abide by them.

In a move to encourage more people to let out rooms in their home, the government allows you to earn up to £4,250 a year free of tax. Any excess rental income you receive over £4,250 will be assessed for tax in the normal way. For further information, see leaflet IR 87 *Letting a Room in Your Home*, available from any tax office. Finally, if you have a mortgage or are a tenant yourself (even with a very long lease), check with your building society or landlord that you are entitled to sublet.

Paying guests or lodgers. This is the most informal arrangement, and will normally be either a casual holiday-type bed-and-breakfast let or a lodger who might be with you for a couple of years. In either case, the visitor would be sharing part of your home, the accommodation would be fully furnished, and you would be providing at least one full meal a day and possibly also basic cleaning services.

There are few legal formalities involved in these types of letting and rent is entirely a matter for friendly agreement. As a resident owner you are also in a very strong position if you want your lodger to leave. Lodging arrangements can easily be ended, as your lodger has no legal rights to stay after the agreed period. A wise precaution would be to check with your insurance company that your home contents policy would not be affected, since some insurers restrict cover to households with lodgers. Also, unless you make arrangements to the contrary, you should inform your lodger that his/her possessions are not covered by your policy.

NB. If, as opposed to a lodger or the occasional summer paying guest, you offer regular B&B accommodation, you could be liable to pay business rates. Although this is not new, it appears that in recent years the Valuation Office Agency has been enforcing the regulation more strictly against people running B&B establishments.

Holiday lets. It is a good idea to register with your tourist information centre and to contact the environmental health office at your local council for any help and advice.

Useful reading

Want to Rent a Room? housing leaflet available from local libraries, housing advice centres and Citizens Advice Bureaux.

The Complete Guide to Letting Property by Liz Hodgkinson, published by Kogan Page, £10.99.

Letting rooms in your home

You could convert a basement or part of your house into a self-contained flat and let this either furnished or unfurnished. Alternatively, you could let a single room or rooms. As a general rule, provided you continue to live in the house your tenant/s would have little security of tenure and equally would not have the right to appeal against the rent. Whether you are letting part of the house as a flat, or simply a room to a lodger, you would be advised to check your home contents policy with your insurance company. For more details, see the housing booklet *Letting Rooms in Your Home – A guide for resident landlords* available from The Department for Communities and Local Government, website: www.communities.gov.uk.publications/housing; Tel: 020 7944 4400; e-mail contactus@communities.gov.uk.

As a resident landlord, you have a guaranteed right to repossession of your property. If the letting was for a fixed term (eg six months or a year), the let will automatically cease at the end of that fixed period. If the arrangement was on a more ad hoc basis with no specified leaving date, it may be legally necessary to give at least four weeks' notice in writing. The position over notices to quit will vary according to circumstances. For further information, see housing booklet *Notice That You Must Leave*, available from The Department for Communities and Local Government. Should you encounter any difficulties, it is possible that you may need to apply to the courts for an eviction order.

Tax note. If you subsequently sell your home, you may not be able to claim exemption from capital gains tax on the increase in value of a flat if it is entirely self-contained. It is therefore a good idea to retain some means of access to the main house or flat, but take legal advice as to what will qualify.

Renting out your home on a temporary basis

If you are thinking of spending the winter in the sun or are considering buying a retirement home that you will not occupy for a year or two, you might be tempted by the idea of letting the whole house. In spite of the changes in the 1996 Housing Act, there are plenty of horror stories of owners who cannot regain possession of their own property when they wish to return.

For your protection, you need to understand the assured shorthold tenancy rules. Unless notified in advance that you need the property back sooner (there are very few grounds on which you can make this notification) or unless earlier possession is sought because of the tenant's behaviour, your tenant would have the right to stay for at least six months and must be given two months' notice before you want the tenancy to end.

It is strongly advisable to ask a solicitor or letting agent to help you draw up the agreement. Although this provides for greater protection, you will probably still require a court possession order if your tenant will not leave after you have given the required amount of notice. The accelerated possession procedure may help in some cases to speed up the process.

In most circumstances, by far the safest solution if possible is to let your property to a company rather than to private individuals, since company tenants do not have the same security of tenure. However, it is important that the contract should make clear that your let is for residential, not business, purposes. Before entering into any agreement, you might find it useful to obtain a copy of booklet *Assured and Assured Shorthold Tenancies – A guide for landlords*, available from your local housing department, or from the DCLG: Tel: 0870 122 6236; e-mail: contactus@communi ties.gov.uk; website: www.communities.gov.uk (**NB**. The leaflet is about letting to individuals – not companies.).

Holiday lets

Buying a future retirement home in the country and renting it out as a holiday home in the summer months is another option worth considering. As well as providing you with a weekend cottage at other times of the year and the chance to establish yourself and make friends in the area, it can also prove a useful and profitable investment.

As long as certain conditions are met, income from furnished holiday lettings enjoys most – but not all – of the benefits that there would be if it were taxed as trading income rather than as investment income. In practical terms, this means that you can claim 25 per cent written-down capital allowances on such items as carpets, curtains and furniture as well as fixtures and fittings, thereby reducing the initial cost of equipping the house. This allowance is being reduced to 10 per cent, which will hit property owners badly. Alternatively, you can claim an annual 10 per cent wear and tear allowance. Running expenses of a holiday home, including maintenance, advertising, insurance cover and council tax (or business rates, see below) are all largely allowable for tax, excluding that element that relates to your own occupation of the property. Since independent taxation was introduced, married couples should consider whether the property be held in the husband's name, the wife's name, or owned jointly. A solicitor or accountant would be able to advise you.

To qualify as furnished holiday accommodation, the property must be situated in the United Kingdom, be let on a commercial basis, be available for holiday letting for at least 140 days during the tax year and be actually let for at least 70 days. Moreover, for at least seven months a year, not necessarily continuous, the property must not normally be occupied by the same tenant for more than 31 consecutive days. This still leaves you with plenty of time to enjoy the property yourself.

The usual word of warning, however: there is always the danger that you might create an assured tenancy, so do take professional advice on drawing up the letting agreement. Similarly, if you decide to use one of the holiday rental agents to market your property, get a solicitor to check any contract you enter into with the company. **RICS (Royal Institution of Chartered Surveyors)**: Tel: 0870 333 1600; website: www.rics.org has a useful set of guidelines for managing agents called *Code of Practice for Management of Residential Property*.

A further point to note is that tax inspectors are taking a tougher line as to what is 'commercial' and that loss-making ventures are being threatened with withdrawal of their tax advantages. To safeguard yourself, it is important to draw up a broad business plan before you start and to make a real effort to satisfy the minimum-letting requirements. In particular, you should be aware that HM Revenue & Customs has been targeting landlords in the belief that many have been failing to declare their rental income or have over-calculated the amount of tax relief to which they are entitled. Even for innocent mistakes, the likely penalty is the same sum as the amount of tax due – so, if you owe £1,000, it could cost you £2,000.

Tenants' deposits. The Tenancy Deposit Scheme came into force in April 2007 and affects all landlords who let-out property under an assured shorthold tenancy. Its purpose is variously to ensure tenants get back the amount owing to them, to make any disputes about the deposit easier to resolve and to encourage tenants to look after the property during the agreed term of their let. The big difference as a result of this new law is that, instead of simply holding the deposit until all or part of it is due to be returned, landlords or agents must now protect it under an approved scheme. Failure to do so within 14 days of receiving the money could result in the landlord being forced to pay the tenant three times the deposit amount.

Landlords and agents have a choice of three approved scheme providers: two of which are insurance-based schemes – Tenancy Deposit Solutions Ltd and the Tenancy Deposit Scheme – and one, The Deposit Protection Service, which provides what is known as custodial deposit protection. With insurance-based schemes, landlords keep the deposit but pay the scheme to insure against their failing to repay the tenant any money due to him/her. The custodial service is free but requires the landlord to put the deposit into the scheme at the start of the tenancy, where it is held until such time as any money is due to be repaid.

In the event of a dispute over the return of the deposit, the custodial scheme will continue to hold the disputed amount until the Alternative Dispute Resolution (ADR) service or the courts decide what is fair. With insurance-based schemes, the disputed amount must be handed over to the scheme for safekeeping until the amount is resolved by the scheme's ADR service. Both types of ADR service are free to the landlord.

The telephone numbers of the three schemes are: **The Deposit Protection Service**: Tel: 0870 707 1707; **Tenancy Deposit Solutions Ltd**: Tel: 0871 703 0055; the **Tenancy Deposit Scheme**: Tel: 0845 226 7837. Or for further information, visit the government website at www.direct.gov. uk/en/Tenancydeposit.

Finally, property that is rented 'commercially' (ie 140 days or more a year) is normally liable for business rates, instead of the council tax you would otherwise pay. This could be more expensive, even though partially allowable against tax.

Useful reading

Housing booklets *Letting Rooms in Your Home* and *Notice That You Must Leave* are available from local authority housing departments or the DCLG: Tel: 0870 122 6236; e-mail: contactus@communities.gov.uk; website: www.com munities.gov.uk.

6

Benefits and taxes

Housing benefit

Provided you have no more than £16,000 in savings, you may be able to get help with your rent from your local council. You may qualify for housing benefit whether you are a council or private tenant or live in a hotel or hostel. Housing benefit is fairly complicated. The following outline is intended only as a very general guide. For more detailed advice about your own particular circumstances, contact your local authority or your Citizens Advice Bureau or Age Concern group.

The amount of benefit you get depends on five factors: the number of people in your household; your eligible rent (up to a prescribed maximum); your capital or savings; your income; and your 'applicable amount', which is the amount of money the government considers you need for basic living expenses. These are defined roughly as follows.

Eligible rent. This includes rent and some service charges related to the accommodation but excludes meals, water rates and, as a rule, fuel costs. An amount will generally also be deducted for any adult 'non-dependant' (including an elderly relative) living in your household, based on a reasonable contribution on their part towards housing costs. This does not apply to commercial boarders or sub-tenants – but any income from a boarder or sub-tenant will be taken into account.

Capital. Any capital or savings up to £6,000 will be disregarded and will not affect your entitlement to benefit. People with savings or capital between £6,000 and £16,000 will receive some benefit but this will be on a sliding scale – with every £500 (or part of £500) over £6,000 assessed as being equivalent to an extra £1 a week of their income. (See paragraph below, starting 'If your income is less than your applicable amount'.) This is called 'tariff income'. If you have savings of more than £16,000 you will not be eligible for housing benefit at all. 'Capital' generally includes all savings, bonds, stocks and shares, and property other than your own home and personal possessions. The capital limits are the same for a couple as for a single person.

Income. Income includes earnings, social security benefits, pension income and any other money you have coming in after tax and National Insurance contributions have been paid. Although most income counts when calculating your entitlement to housing benefit (**NB** a couple's income is added together), some income may be ignored, for example all disability living allowance and attendance allowance; the first £5 of earnings (single person), £10 of earnings (couple) or £20 of earnings if your 'applicable amount' includes a disability premium or carer's premium; there is £25 disregard for lone parents; war pensions are also ignored in part.

Applicable amount. Your 'applicable amount' will generally be the same as any benefit to cover weekly living expenses you would be eligible for and consists of: your personal allowance, personal allowances for any younger children (normally those for whom you are receiving child benefit), plus any premiums (ie additional amounts for pensioners, the disabled and so on) to which you might be entitled. Details of allowances and premium rates are contained in leaflet GL23 available from any housing benefit office.

If your income is less than your 'applicable amount', you will receive maximum housing benefit towards your eligible rent (less any non-dependant deduction). You may be eligible for income support if your capital is less than £8,000, or less than £16,000 if you are aged 60 or over. If your income is equal to your 'applicable amount', you will also receive maximum housing benefit. If your income is higher than your 'applicable amount', a taper adjustment will be made and maximum housing benefit will be reduced by 65 per cent of the difference between your income and your 'applicable amount'. If this leaves you with housing benefit of less than 50p a week, it is not paid.

How to claim. If you think you are eligible for benefit (see leaflets GL16 and GL17 available from any housing benefit office), ask your council for an application form. It should let you know within 14 days of receiving your completed application whether you are entitled to benefit, and will inform you of the amount. Websites: www.dwp.gov.uk and www.direct.gov.uk.

Special accommodation. If you live in a mobile home or houseboat, you may be able to claim benefit for site fees or mooring charges. If you live in a private nursing or residential care home you will not normally be able to get housing benefit to help with the cost. However, you may be able to get help towards both the accommodation part of your fees and your living expenses through income support or possibly under the community care arrangements. If you make a claim for income support, you can claim housing benefit and council tax benefit at the same time. A claim form for these is included inside the income support claim form. When completed, the form is returned to your local authority.

Useful reading

Leaflet RR2 *A Guide to Housing Benefit and Council Tax Benefit*, free from your council.

Housing Benefit and Council Tax Benefit, free factsheet from Age Concern: T: 0800 00 99 66; website: www.age concern.org.uk.

Council tax

Council tax is based on the value of the dwelling in which

you live (the property element) and also consists of a personal element – with discounts/exemptions applying to certain groups of people.

The property element

Most domestic properties are liable for council tax, including rented property, mobile homes and houseboats. The value of the property is assessed according to a banding system, with eight different bands (A to H), ranging in England from property valued at up to £40,000 (band A) to property valued at over £320,000 (band H). In Wales, the bands run from up to £44,000 (band A) to over £424,000 (band I). In Scotland, the bands run from up to £27,000 (band A) to over £212,000 (band H).

The banding of each property is determined by the government's Valuation Office Agency based on prices applying at 1 April 1991, except for Wales where revaluation took effect in April 2003. Small extensions or other improvements made after this date do not affect the valuation until the property changes hands. New homes in England and Scotland are banded as if they had already been built and sold on 1 April 1991, in order to be consistent. The planned council tax revaluation in England, due to take place in 2007, has been postponed.

Notification of the band is shown on the bill when it is sent out in April. If you think there has been a misunderstanding about the valuation (or your liability to pay the full amount) you may have the right of appeal (see 'Appeals', page 83).

Liability

Not everyone pays council tax. The bill is normally sent to the resident owner or joint owners of the property, or in the case of rented accommodation, to the tenant or joint tenants. Married couples and people with a shared legal interest in the property are jointly liable for the bill, unless they are students or severely mentally impaired. In some cases, for example in hostels or multi-occupied property, a non-resident landlord or owner will be liable but may pass on a share of the bill to the tenants/residents, which would probably be included as part of the rental charge.

The personal element

The valuation of each dwelling assumes that two adults will be resident. The charge does not increase if there are more adults. However, if, as in many homes, there is a single adult, your council tax bill will be reduced by 25 per cent. Certain people are disregarded when determining the number of residents in a household. There are also a number of other special discounts, or exemptions, as follows:

■ People who are severely mentally impaired are disregarded, or if they are the sole occupant of the dwelling, qualify for an exemption.

■ Disabled people whose homes require adaptation may have their bill reduced to a lower band.

■ People on income support should normally have nothing to pay, as their bill will be met in full by council tax benefit.

■ Disabled people on higher rate attendance allowance need not count a full-time carer as an additional resident and therefore may continue to qualify for the 25 per cent single (adult) householder discount. Exceptions are spouses/partners and parents of a disabled child under 18 who would normally be living with the disabled person and whose presence therefore would not be adding to the council tax.

■ Young people over 18 but still at school are not counted when assessing the number of adults in a house.

■ Students living in halls of residence, student hostels or similar are exempted; those living with a parent or other non-student adult are eligible for the 25 per cent personal discount.

■ Service personnel living in barracks or married quarters will not receive any bill for council tax.

Discounts/exemptions applying to property

Certain property is either exempt from council tax or is eligible for a discount.

Discounts. Until April 2004, there was a standard 50 per cent discount on second homes and long-term empty property (except in Wales, where councils could charge the full amount on second homes if they wished). However, you can no longer count on this as in England councils now have the power to charge owners of second homes up to 90 per cent of the standard rate; and owners of long-term empty property up to 100 per cent.

Exemptions. The most common cases of exemptions include:

■ Property that has been unoccupied and unfurnished for less than six months.

■ Home of a deceased person: the exemption lasts until six months after the grant of probate.

■ Home that is empty because the occupier is absent in order to care for someone else.

■ Home of a person who is/would be exempted from council tax due to moving to a residential home, hospital care or similar.

■ Empty properties in need of major repairs or undergoing structural alteration can be exempt from council tax for an initial period of six months and this can be extended for a further six months. After 12 months, the standard 50 (or possibly full 100) per cent charge for empty properties will apply.

■ Granny flats that are part of another private domestic dwelling may be exempt, but this depends on access and other conditions. To check, contact your local Valuation Office.

Business-cum-domestic property

Business-cum-domestic property is rated according to usage, with the business section assessed for business rates and the domestic section for council tax. For example, where there is a flat over a shop, the value of the shop would not be included in the valuation for council tax. Likewise, a room in a house used for business purposes would be subject to business rates and not to council tax.

Appeals

If you become the new person responsible for paying the council tax (eg, because you have recently moved or because someone else paid the tax before) on a property that you feel has been wrongly banded, you have six months to appeal and can request that the valuation be reconsidered. Otherwise, there are only three other circumstances in which you can appeal. These are: 1) if there has been a material increase or reduction in the property's value; 2) if you start, or stop, using part of the property for business or the balance between domestic and business use changes; 3) if either of the latter two apply and the listing officer has altered the council tax list without giving you a chance to put your side.

If you have grounds for appeal, you should take up the matter with the valuation office (see local telephone directory). If the matter is not resolved, you can then appeal to an independent valuation tribunal. For advice and further information, contact your local Citizens Advice Bureau.

Useful reading

Council Tax: A guide to your bill and *Council Tax: A guide to valuation, banding and appeals*, obtainable free from any council office or from the DCLG: Tel: 0870 122 6236; e-mail: contactus@communities.gov.uk; website: www.com munities.gov.uk.

Council tax benefit

If you cannot afford your council tax because you have a low income, you may be able to obtain council tax benefit. The help is more generous than many people realise. For example, people on pension credit (guarantee credit) are entitled to rebates of up to 100 per cent. Even if you are not receiving any other social security benefit, you may still qualify for some council tax benefit. The amount you get depends on your income, savings, your personal circumstances, who else lives in your home (in particular whether they would be counted as a 'non-dependant') and on your net council tax bill (ie after any deductions that apply to your home). If you are not sure whether your income is low enough to entitle you to council tax benefit, it is worth making a claim, as you could be pleasantly surprised.

If you disagree with your council's decision, you can ask for this to be looked at again (a revision) or you can appeal to an independent appeal tribunal, administered by the Appeals Service. If you are still dissatisfied, you may apply for leave to appeal to the Social Security Commissioners, but only on a point of law. If you want a revision, you should get on with the matter as soon as possible, because if you delay your request may be out of time.

Apart from council tax benefit for yourself, you may also be able to get help with your council tax if you share your home with someone who is on a low income. This is known as second adult rebate, or alternative maximum council tax benefit. For further information, ask your local council for leaflet GL17 *Help With Your Council Tax*. As well as the English version, this is available in 11 other languages.

Useful organisations

The following should be able to provide general advice about housing and help with housing problems:

▓ local authority housing departments;

▓ housing advice or housing aid centres;

▓ Citizens Advice Bureaux;

▓ local authority social service departments if your problem is linked to disability;

▓ welfare rights centres if your problem, for example, concerns a landlord who does not keep the property properly maintained;

▓ leasehold valuation tribunals if there are serious problems with the management of the building;

▓ local councillors and MPs.

Other organisations that provide a helpful service are:

CHAS Central London. CHAS serves anyone in acute housing need regardless of race or religion. It provides free information, advice and advocacy on housing, homelessness, debt and welfare benefits issues. Tel: 020 7723 5928; e-mail: chascl@chascl.org.uk; website: www.chascl.org.uk.

Federation of Private Residents' Associations Ltd (FPRA) is a federation of associations of long-leaseholders and tenants in private blocks of flats. It advises on setting up residents' associations and provides legal and other advice to its member associations. It issues a quarterly newsletter and information sheets, publishes a pack on how to form a tenants'/residents' association (price £15 including p&p) and acts as a pressure group seeking to influence legislation regarding leasehold and management of flats in the private sector. FPRA also gives advice on buying the freehold and on management of collectively owned blocks of flats. Tel: 0871 200 3324; e-mail: info@fpra.org.uk; website: www.fpra.org.uk.

Shelter. The National Campaign for Homeless People, Shelter, provides advice to over 100,000 badly housed and homeless people every year through a national network of housing aid centres and a free 24-hour housing helpline. Tel: 0808 800 4444; e-mail: info@shelter.org.uk; website: www.shelter.org.uk.

Useful reading

The Housing and Planning Year Book. This is published

annually in the Longman's Community Information Guide series and will be found in most library reference sections. It lists, among others, all national and local government offices responsible for housing, all national advisory bodies, major house builders, housing associations, professional bodies and trade associations involved with house building. This is an invaluable book for anyone considering the options for retirement housing.

7

The elderly and people with disabilities

Ways of adapting your home

Many even quite elderly people will not require anything more complicated than a few general improvements. These could range from: better lighting, especially near staircases; a non-slip mat and grab-rail in the bathroom; and safer heating arrangements. For some it might be necessary perhaps to lower some kitchen and other units to place them within easy reach.

Another sensible plan worth considering is to convert a downstairs room into a bedroom and bathroom, should managing the stairs later become difficult.

For some people, however, such arrangements are not really sufficient. In the case of a physically handicapped or disabled person, more radical improvements will usually be required. Far from presenting a major problem as used to be the case, today these are normally fairly easy to organise.

Local authority help

Local authorities have a legal duty to help people with disabilities and, depending on what is required and the individual's ability to pay, may assist with the cost. You can either approach your GP or contact the social services department direct. A sympathetic doctor will be able to advise what is needed and supply any prescriptions, such as for a medical hoist. Your GP will also be able to suggest which unit or department to approach as well as make a recommendation to the housing department, should rehousing be desirable.

The social services department may be able to supply kitchen, bathroom and other aids for the home. They can also arrange an appointment with an occupational therapist and support an application for a grant, should major adaptations be required.

If only relatively small changes are necessary, such as a handrail on the stairs or ramp for a wheelchair, the occupational therapist may be able to arrange for these to be done by the local authority. This can take months, however, so if you cannot wait and want the work done privately, the occupational therapist will give you names of local firms.

Help with home repair and adaptations

The Regulatory Reform Order (RRO), gives local authorities greater discretionary powers to provide assistance – such as low-cost loans and grants – to help with renovations, repairs and adaptations to the home. If it is more appropriate, it is also empowered to help someone move to more suitable accommodation. In particular, the RRO replaces the previous legislation governing renovation grant, common parts grant, HMO grant and home repair assistance. It allows local authorities greater flexibility to determine their particular eligibility criteria, whether means testing should be involved and also the type of assistance available. Any assistance given, however, must be in accordance with the authority's published policy. For further information contact the environmental health or housing department of your local authority. See website: www.berr.gov.uk.

Disabled facilities grant (DFG). This is designed to adapt or provide facilities for a home (including the common parts where applicable) to make it more suitable for occupation by a disabled person. It can cover a wide range of improvements to enable the disabled to manage more independently. These include work to facilitate access either to the property itself or to the main rooms, the provision of suitable bathroom or kitchen facilities, the adaptation of heating or lighting controls, improvement of the heating system and various other works where these would make a home safe for a disabled person. Provided the applicant is eligible, a mandatory grant of up to £25,000 in England may be available. For further information and application form, contact the environmental health or housing department of your local authority, see website: www.direct.gov.uk/Disabled People/.

Home improvement agencies (HIAs)

HIAs are small not-for-profit organisations that assist older, disabled and vulnerable homeowners, or private sector tenants, to repair, maintain or adapt their homes. Many also give advice about benefits and operate schemes for energy efficiency, crime prevention and other ways of making a home safer and more comfortable. By improving people's living conditions, HIAs enhance their quality of life and enable them to remain in their home in greater comfort and security. For details of your nearest HIA it would be sensible to contact the national coordinating body for HIAs, whose website provides a directory of home improvement agencies and the services each provides. If there is no HIA in your area, you might usefully try contacting your local authority, Citizens Advice Bureau or Age Concern Group.

Foundations. Tel: 01457 891909; e-mail: foundations@cel. co.uk; website: www.foundations.uk.com.

Other sources of help

DEMAND (Design & Manufacture for Disability) can design and make individual items of furniture and equipment, or modify existing products, for people with particular needs where there is nothing suitable available elsewhere. For further information contact: Tel: 01923 681800; website: www.demand.org.uk.

The **Disabled Living Foundation (DLF)** is a charity concerned with the practical daily living problems of disability. As well as running a telephone enquiry service, DLF has an equipment centre where gadgets of all kinds can be demonstrated and tried out by visitors. The range includes: special equipment for the bathroom, kitchen, bedroom and living room; hoists, wheelchairs and gadgets to assist reading and writing. None of the items is for sale but the centre can provide information on suppliers and prices. The centre is staffed by information advisers who show visitors round and discuss individual needs. To arrange an appointment, contact: Tel: 0845 130 9177; e-mail: info@dlf.org.uk; website: www.dlf.org.uk.

Assist UK heads up a UK-wide network of locally situated Disabled Living Centres. Each centre includes a permanent exhibition of products and equipment that provides people with an opportunity to see and try them and get information and advice from professional staff. There are over 325 advisors working at over 60 member centres. Assist UK is the only organisation in the United Kingdom to connect clients, manufacturers, regulators and professionals. For details of your nearest centre, contact the headquarters on: Tel: 0870 770 2866; e-mail: general.info@assist-uk.org; website: www.assist-uk.org.

Both the **British Red Cross** (www.redcross.org.uk) and **Age Concern** (www.AgeConcern.org.uk) can loan equipment in the short term and may also be able to advise on local stockists. Larger branches of Boots, for example, sell a wide range of special items for people with disabilities, including bath aids, wheelchairs and crutches.

Keep Able operates a chain of 28 specialist shops across the country, which stock a wide range of gadgets and equipment to make life easier for elderly and less-able people. Professional advice is available in all the shops and home visits can be arranged without obligation. A free mail-order catalogue is available. For further information, contact: Tel: 08705 20 21 22/0844 888 1338; e-mail: customerservices@keepable.co.uk; website: www.keepable.co.uk.

REMAP can often help design or adapt goods to suit individuals where there is no commercially available product to meet their particular needs. For further information, contact: Tel: 0845 130 0456; website: www.remap.org.uk.

The **Centre for Accessible Environments** runs the House Adaptations Advisory Service and can recommend local architects with experience of designing for disabled people. When contacting them, you should give broad details of the type of work required. For further details, contact: Tel: 020 7840 0125; e-mail: info@cae.org.uk; website: www.cae.org. uk.

Another useful body to know about is **OFCOM,** which operates a complaints line for consumers who have a complaint about their telecom company that they are unable to resolve with either the company or with the Ombudsman. Tel: 020 7981 3040; website: www.ofcom.org.uk.

Another helpful source of advice is **Disability Wales/ Anabledd Cymru,** contact: Tel: 029 2088 7325, e-mail: info@disabilitywales.org; website: www.disabilitywales.org.

Alarm systems

Alarm systems have become much more widespread in recent years. The knowledge that help can be summoned quickly in the event of an emergency is reassuring in its own right to many elderly or disabled people. In practical terms it can enable many people to remain independent far longer than would otherwise be sensible. Some local authorities have alarm systems that now allow people living in their own homes to be linked to a central control. Types of alarm vary greatly. Some have a telephone link, enabling personal contact to be made. Others simply signal that something is wrong. In other systems, a relative or friend who has been nominated will be alerted, or sometimes the alarm will go through to the police. To find out whether your local authority operates such a system, contact the social services department: website: www.dh.gov.uk.

Commercial firms

A number of firms install and operate alarm systems. Price, installation cost and reliability can vary quite considerably. For advice on choosing an alarm plus a list of suppliers, contact the **Disabled Living Foundation**: Tel: 0845 130 9177; e-mail: info@dlf.org.uk; website: www.dlf.org.uk.

Community alarms

Telephone alarm systems operated on the public telephone network can be used by anyone with a direct telephone line. The systems link into a 24-hour monitoring centre and have a pendant that enables help to be called even when the owner is some distance from the telephone. Grants may be available in some cases to meet the costs. One of the most widely used systems is SeniorLink, run by Help the Aged. For further information, contact **SeniorLink Enquiry Line**: Tel: 0845 603 4576; e-mail: info@helptheaged.org.uk; website: www.helptheaged.org.uk.

Age Concern Aid-Call

This is another highly recommended alarm system. The subscriber has a small radio transmitter, worn as a pendant or like a watch, which contacts a 24-hour monitoring centre. The centre then alerts a list of nominated relatives or friends, or the emergency services, that something is wrong. Help can be on its way in a matter of minutes. For more details, contact **Age Concern Aid-Call**: Tel: 0800 77 22 66; e-mail: info@aidcall-alarms.co.uk; website: www.aidcall.co.uk.

Main local authority services

Quite apart from any assistance with housing, local authorities supply a number of services that can prove invaluable to an elderly person. The two most important are meals on wheels and home helps. Additionally, there are social workers and various specialists concerned with aspects of health. Since the introduction of Community Care, local authority social services departments have taken over all responsibility for helping to assess and coordinate the best arrangements for individuals according to their particular requirements.

Meals on wheels

The meals on wheels service is sometimes run by local authorities direct and sometimes by voluntary organisations, such as WRVS, acting as their agents. As you know, the purpose is to deliver a hot lunch (or batch of frozen lunches) to individuals in their own homes. Different arrangements apply in different areas and schemes variously operate from two to seven days a week, or possibly less frequently when frozen meals are supplied. Cost also varies, from about £2 to £4 a day, with the norm being about £2.50. For further information, contact the social services department.

WRVS also runs a private frozen meals scheme that delivers complete frozen meals direct to customers' doors. The price of a three-course meal ranges from £4.35 to £5.50. For further information, call Tel: 0845 601 4670; website: www. wrvs.org.uk.

Home helps

Local authorities have a legal obligation to run a home help service to help frail and housebound elderly people with such basic household chores as shopping, tidying up, a little light cooking and so on. In many areas the service is badly overstretched, so the amount of help actually available varies considerably, as does the method of charging. Different local authorities have different policies and although some may charge nothing or just a small weekly amount, as a rule people are means-tested according to their ability to pay. If you could afford to do so, this could mean paying the full cost. Apply through the social services department. Some of the larger authorities have a special telephone number that may be listed either as 'Home help services' or 'Domiciliary services': website: www.dh.gov.uk.

Specialist helpers

Local authorities employ a number of specialist helpers, variously based in the social services department or health centre, who are there to assist.

Social workers. Normally the first people to contact if you have a problem. They can put you in touch with the right person, if you require a home help, meals on wheels, have a housing difficulty or have another query and are not sure whom to approach. Often, even if ultimately it is the responsibility of another department, a social worker may come and discuss the matter with you. You should ring the social services department; in Scotland, this is normally referred to as the social work department.

Occupational therapists have a wide knowledge of disability and can assist individuals via training, exercise, or access to aids, equipment or adaptations to the home. Ring the social services department.

Health visitors. Qualified nurses with broad knowledge both of health matters and of the various services available through the local authority. Rather like social workers, health visitors can put you in touch with whatever specialised facilities are required. Contact through the local health centre.

District nurses. Fully qualified nurses who will visit a patient in the home, change dressings, attend to other routine nursing matters, monitor progress and help with the arrangements if more specialised care is required. Contact through the health centre.

Physiotherapists. Use exercise and massage to help improve mobility and strengthen muscles, for example after an operation or to alleviate a crippling condition. Normally available at both hospitals and health centres.

Medical social workers (MSWs). In the old days, these used to be known as almoners. They are available to consult if patients have any problems – whether practical or emotional – on leaving hospital. MSWs can advise on coping with a disablement, as well as such practical matters as transport, after-care and other immediate arrangements. They work in hospitals and an appointment should be made before the patient is discharged.

Good neighbour schemes

A number of local authorities have an organised system of good neighbour schemes. In essence, these consist of individuals contracting with the authority to act as good neighbours to one or several elderly people living close by. Depending on what is required, they may simply pop in on a daily basis to check that everything is all right, or they may give more sustained assistance such as providing help with dressing, bathing, shopping or preparing a light meal. In some authorities, the service may largely be run by volunteer organisations; in others, 'good neighbours' are paid by the authority according to the number of hours they commit. To find out whether such a scheme exists locally, enquire at the social services department.

Key voluntary organisations

Voluntary organisations complement the services provided by statutory health and social services in making life easier for elderly people living at home. The range of provision varies from area to area but can include:

■ lunch clubs;

■ holidays and short-term placements;

■ day centres and clubs;

■ friendly visiting;

■ aids such as wheelchairs;

■ transport;

■ odd jobs and decorating;

▤ gardening;

▤ good-neighbour schemes;

▤ prescription collection;

▤ advice and information;

▤ family support schemes.

The particular organisation providing these services depends on where you live but the Citizens Advice Bureau (website: www.citizensadvice.org.uk) will be able to advise you whom to contact. The following are the key agencies:

Age Concern may provide any or all of the voluntary services listed above in your local area. Many local groups recruit volunteers to do practical jobs and provide friendship. They also give advice and information and when necessary refer enquirers to a more appropriate agency.

Age Concern England: Tel: 0800 00 99 66; website: www. ageconcern.org.uk.

Age Concern Scotland: Tel: 0845 125 9732; website: www. ageconcernscotland.org.uk.

Age Concern Cymru: Tel: 029 2043 1555; website: www. accymru.org.uk.

Age Concern Northern Ireland: Tel: 028 9024 5729; website: www.ageconcernni.org.

WRVS runs many local projects:

■ books-on-wheels;

■ social transport;

■ meals on wheels;

■ good neighbour schemes;

■ lunch clubs;

■ Darby and Joan clubs;

■ meal delivery service for those not qualifying for meals on wheels.

For further information, contact **WRVS**: Tel: 01235 442900; website: www.wrvs.org.uk.

British Red Cross supplies some important services to elderly people. The principal ones available from many branches include:

■ helping sick, disabled or frail people make essential journeys;

■ loaning medical equipment for short-term use at home and on holiday;

■ providing home-from-hospital support: easing the transition of patients to their own home after discharge and giving support to both them and their carers;

▪ 'signposting' vulnerable people towards the statutory or voluntary services from which their needs may best be met.

To contact the **British Red Cross (BRCS)**: Tel: 0844 871 11 11; e-mail: information@redcross.org.uk; website: www. red-cross.org.uk.

St John Ambulance has over 45,000 volunteers who provide first aid and care services. They help in hospitals and in some areas will also come to people's homes to assist with various practical tasks such as shopping, collecting pensions, staying with an elderly person for a few hours or providing transport to and from hospital. It is emphasised, however, that the kind of help that the volunteers can provide (if any) varies enormously from county to county and depends on the local resources available. In some areas loan of equipment such as wheelchairs can be arranged.

St John Ambulance gives advice on caring and runs courses locally for carers looking after elderly people. Anyone wishing to enlist the help of St John Ambulance should contact the national headquarters: **St John Ambulance**: Tel: 020 7324 4000; website: www.sja.org.uk.

Other sources of help and advice

Counsel & Care provides a free confidential advisory service for older people and their relatives. Advice workers liaise with all the statutory services, and private and voluntary organisations. They also work with charities and benevolent funds to inform families of the various options. There is a range of factsheets. Limited funds are also available to help with an exceptional-needs payment. For further information, contact: Tel: 0845 300 7585; e-mail: advice@counselandcare.org.uk; website: www.counselandcare.org.uk.

Jewish Care provides services for elderly Jewish people, including those who are mentally ill, in London and the South East. Principal facilities include: special day-care centres for people with dementia; residential and nursing homes in North London, Redbridge, Brighton and Southend; community centres; a home-care service for the housebound and short-term respite care to give carers a break or to give frail, elderly people the opportunity of a short holiday, particularly during the Jewish festivals. There is also a Kosher meals-on-wheels service. Enquire through the local authority social services department or contact Jewish Care head office for further information: Tel: 020 8922 2222; e-mail: jcdirect@jcare.org; website: www. jewishcare.org.

Help the Aged runs SeniorLine, a free advice and information service, available throughout the United Kingdom for older people and their carers. Trained advice workers can help with enquiries about welfare/disability benefits, community/residential care and housing options. Contact: Tel: 020 7278 1114; website: www.helptheaged.org.uk. **Help The Aged England, Scotland and Wales:** Tel: 0808 800 6565. **Help The Aged Northern Ireland:** Tel: 0808 808 7575.

The Civil Service Retirement Fellowship runs a home visiting service for those who are housebound or living alone. It has an extensive network of branches and local groups throughout the country. These offer a wide range of social activities for retired civil servants, their partners and dependants. For further information, contact: Tel: 020 8691 7411; website: www.csrf.org.uk.

Disability Alliance publishes a number of free factsheets and also an annual *Disability Rights Handbook*, which is packed with information on benefits and services for all people with disabilities and their families. For further information, contact: Tel: 020 7247 8776; e-mail: office.da@dial.pipex. com; website: www.disabilityalliance.org.

Stop press

Help with mortgages

For those finding it difficult to maintain mortgage payments, the Government secured commitment from mortgage lenders to wait at least three months after a borrower falls behind with their repayments before seeking repossession.

Also, from January 2009 anyone who loses their job who has a mortgage of up to £200,000 is eligible for a state benefit. This benefit pays the interest on their mortgage, allowing people to remain in their homes. The current cap to be eligible for this benefit (called Income Support for Mortgage Interest) is £100,000.

Help with insulation

An extra £100 million is to be provided, with a further £50 million brought forward, to help 60,000 more households insulate their homes.

Debt advice

The government will provide an extra £15 million for the provision of debt advice.

Summary

Hopefully, your retirement will be long, healthy and happy. In order to maximise the chances of this it pays to spend time considering whether where you live now, and how you live now, are practical – will things need to change in the future, and if so, what options there are available for you. If you and your spouse are healthy you may have years of active life ahead of you, but there is the possibility (as happens to a number of people) that you may take on the care of an elderly relative.

The preceding information should give you some useful sources of advice whatever your personal circumstances. With a bit of time spent taking stock of whether you are where you want to be, and what can be done to improve things if needed, your home life should be trouble-free and enjoyable for the foreseeable future.

Notes

ALSO AVAILABLE FROM KOGAN PAGE

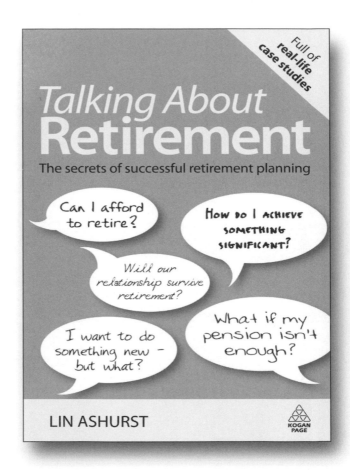

ISBN: 978 0 7494 5515 6   Paperback   2009

ALSO AVAILABLE FROM KOGAN PAGE

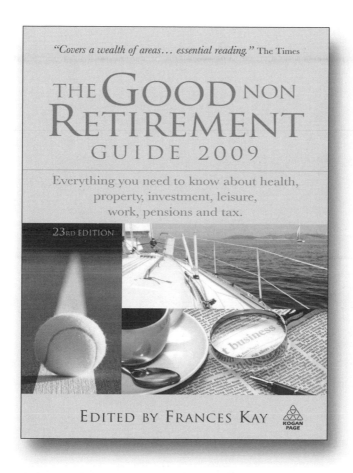

"Covers a wealth of areas… essential reading." The Times

THE GOOD NON RETIREMENT GUIDE 2009

Everything you need to know about health, property, investment, leisure, work, pensions and tax.

23RD EDITION

EDITED BY FRANCES KAY

ISBN: 978 0 7494 5272 8   Paperback   2009